Shakespeare's Tragedies
Part I

Professor Clare R. Kinney

THE TEACHING COMPANY ®

PUBLISHED BY:

THE TEACHING COMPANY
4151 Lafayette Center Drive, Suite 100
Chantilly, Virginia 20151-1232
1-800-TEACH-12
Fax—703-378-3819
www.teach12.com

ISBN 978-1-59803-309-0

Clare R. Kinney, Ph.D.
Associate Professor of English, University of Virginia

Clare R. Kinney is British by birth and earned her B.A. in English at Cambridge University. A Paul W. Mellon Fellowship brought her to Yale University, where she received her Ph.D. After first teaching at Yale, she moved in 1985 to the University of Virginia, where she specializes in the literature of the English Renaissance and occasionally teaches medieval literature. She has served as Associate Chair and Director of Undergraduate Studies in the UVA English Department and is currently in charge of its Distinguished Majors Program.

Professor Kinney's many scholarly articles include essays on Shakespeare, Christopher Marlowe, Edmund Spenser, Philip Sidney, Lady Mary Wroth, Chaucer, the Gawain poet, and other Renaissance and medieval authors; she has also written on the teaching of earlier English literature. Her book, *Strategies of Poetic Narrative: Chaucer, Spenser, Milton, Eliot*, was published by Cambridge University Press in 1992. An occasional actress, she has participated in staged readings of lesser-known plays by Shakespeare's contemporaries at the reconstructed Blackfriars Theatre in Staunton, Virginia, and she has directed student performances of scenes from Shakespeare in her lecture courses. Professor Kinney has received a Distinguished Faculty Award from the Z Society of the University of Virginia. In 2007 she was the recipient of a University of Virginia All-University Teaching Award.

Table of Contents
Shakespeare's Tragedies
Part I

Shakespeare's Tragedies

Scope:

This course will explore Shakespeare's six mature tragedies: *Hamlet, Othello, King Lear, Macbeth, Antony and Cleopatra,* and *Coriolanus.* (Because the course focus is on the period from 1600 to 1608, in which Shakespeare produced his most compelling tragic dramas, and because it does not address "tragedies of fate," *Romeo and Juliet* is omitted.) The course goals are as follows: to offer an introduction to tragedy as a literary genre and to outline the main characteristics of Shakespearean tragedy; to acquaint students with themes that Shakespeare almost obsessively revisits and reconfigures across the span of the major tragedies; to historicize the plays by suggesting some ways in which they might speak to the anxieties and preoccupations of the playwright's 17th-century audience; to offer detailed and thought-provoking explorations of individual plays on their own terms; and to illustrate the power and audacity of Shakespeare's poetry and stagecraft.

These lectures suggest that Shakespeare's tragedies repeatedly address tensions between the will and desires of the individual and the constraints emanating from his or her society. The plays are consistently interested in the relationship between public and private life and in the emotional fissures within what one might anachronistically call dysfunctional families. Throughout the course, we will examine the different kinds of power under negotiation in Shakespeare's tragic universes: political power, erotic power, the power of language and the imagination, and the power of theater itself ("the play's the thing / Wherein I'll catch the conscience of the king!"). The lectures will also explore the larger philosophical and theological questions raised by Shakespeare's characters when they ask what non-human forces control their universe. Is there providence in the fall of a sparrow, as Hamlet declares—or do the gods kill us for their sport, as the despairing Earl of Gloucester suggests in *King Lear*?

The course will have a lot to say about tragic agency: lectures will consider who does or does not get to make significant choices in the imaginative space of these plays—and who does or does not get to reflect upon their actions. We will also ponder the slippery borderline between action and transgression. We might think of transgression as being coterminous with *tragic* action, and we will keep revisiting the question of what constitutes transgression in Shakespeare's works—what does it mean to overstep the boundaries of permitted action, to challenge the norms of one's society, to put oneself beyond the pale? And why have audiences found the dramatization of that moment of transgression (and its consequences) so consistently fascinating across the centuries? The course will also ask whether women can figure as tragic protagonists in Shakespearean drama (all but one of these plays are named after male heroes): several of the lectures will explore the role played by female transgression in the imaginative economy of the tragedies.

The course is bracketed by three "framing lectures": two preliminary ones setting out literary and historical contexts for reading the plays and a concluding presentation that ends by glancing at what happened when Shakespeare, at the very end of his career, went on to write "beyond tragedy." Of the remaining 21 lectures, the three or four units devoted to each particular play will offer multiple angles of approach to the conflicts it dramatizes and the questions it raises (at times drawing connections with other works addressed in the course). The three presentations on *Macbeth*, for example, include a lecture whose starting point is an exploration of the play's resonant allusions to contemporary controversies and to the uneasy rule of England's new (and Scottish) ruler, James I; a lecture focusing on the play's gender politics and, in particular, its dramatization of competing definitions of heroic manhood; and a lecture focusing on the poetic language and plot action that links Macbeth's desire to control the future (and his preoccupation with royal and dynastic succession) to the lives and deaths of children in the tragedy. All of the lectures on individual plays will balance larger thematic considerations with careful attention to the nuances of the astonishing language in which Shakespeare's tragic protagonists give voice to their alienation and estrangement from ordinary experience—in which, one might say, they speak the unspeakable.

In the earliest surviving analysis of the workings of tragedy, Aristotle's *Poetics*, tragedy is defined not only by its content but by its effect upon an audience: Aristotle speaks of the pity and fear it should evoke and the *catharsis* or purgation it should produce. It is a critical commonplace that the suffering of the tragic protagonist is rendered significant by the special insight or vision it allows him or her to achieve, and these lectures will regularly consider what kind of "tragic knowledge" Shakespeare's protagonists articulate *in extremis*. But they will also look carefully at the larger understanding and emotional engagement experienced by the audiences of these dramas: this course will persist in asking what kind of significance *we*, in the 21st century, might wrest out of Shakespeare's tragic spectacles.

Lecture One
Defining Tragedy

Scope:

Tragic drama, the art of rendering suffering significant, has always been highly valued in Western culture. This lecture explores its persistent popularity, looking at both pre-Shakespearean discussions of tragedy (such as those of Aristotle and Sir Philip Sidney) and more recent theorizations of this literary genre. An introductory survey of some of the issues Shakespeare repeatedly addresses in his six mature tragedies explores the nature of tragic transgression (and critiques the rather reductive notion of the "tragic flaw"). This discussion touches on Shakespeare's particular interest in exploring complicated relationships between the tragic protagonist and his or her family and community; it also introduces the concept of *tragic knowledge*. The lecture concludes with some remarks on the particular challenges and satisfactions offered by Shakespeare's language and idiom.

Outline

I. For more than 2,400 years, writers and audiences in the West have been fascinated with watching reenactments of terrible human suffering and, in particular, the painful experience of someone whom we label a *tragic protagonist*.

    A. The earliest discussion of tragedy is to be found in Aristotle's *Poetics* in the 4th century B.C.E.

        1. Aristotle suggests that tragic drama will be written in elevated language and will deal with a self-contained action.

        2. Its plot will involve dramatic reversals and climactic recognition, or *anagnorisis*, and it will evoke particular emotions (pity and fear) in its audience.

        3. Tragic protagonists are usually elevated by rank and/or ability over most other people and fall victim to *hamartia:* an "error in action" rather than pathological vice.

        4. *Hamartia* is often mistranslated as "tragic flaw"; this is

reductive because the crisis of a tragic protagonist is the product of an extreme combination of internal *and* external forces.

5. Aristotle doesn't only speak of tragic content: his notion of *catharsis* (the purging of certain emotions evoked by the play) also focuses on the response it creates in an audience.

B. Medieval notions of tragedy are often not applied to drama but to narratives in general.

1. Geoffrey Chaucer's *Canterbury Tales* offers a definition of tragedy that primarily emphasizes a fall from greatness to wretchedness.

2. This medieval definition suggests a Christian moral: the reader is encouraged to scorn transient, earthly pleasures and glories.

C. In Renaissance England, Sir Philip Sidney's *Defence of Poetry* offers a somewhat different definition of tragedy.

1. Sidney suggests that tragedy is a didactic form that lays bare the corruption that rulers and statesmen may attempt to conceal.

2. He argues that art, in mirroring nature, can move people to virtuous action with its stirring or admonitory examples.

3. Although Sidney's discussion of tragedy uses quasi-Aristotelian notions of the particular effects it can create, it also echoes the medieval notion that tragedy shows the fragility of earthly splendors.

II. *Tragedy* is not a stable term; it is always being renegotiated. There has, however, been a certain critical consensus about what constitutes Shakespearean tragedy.

A. The experiences of Shakespeare's tragic protagonists—or the consequences of choices they have made—estrange them from ordinary existence.

B. The fall of the tragic protagonist is likely to have reverberations within a whole community.

C. Tragic protagonists generally draw from their suffering a kind of insight that allows them to find some universalizing and higher significance in their experience.

    1. This often speaks to our own attempts to come to terms with the existence of human evil (and addresses our doubt that a benign higher power would permit it to flourish).

    2. Tragedy's particular eminence as a literary genre stems from the value traditionally granted to works of art that attempt to extract some kind of meaning out of human suffering.

  D. It should be recognized, however, that Shakespeare's contemporaries did not themselves define tragedy in this way: it is later writers who suggest that suffering is redeemed in his work because it is made to *signify*.

  E. It is sometimes questionable whether complete understanding is achieved by the characters who participate in a play's tragic action; such understanding may need to be retrospectively constructed by the work's audience.

III. Between 1600 and 1608, Shakespeare wrote the works generally thought of as his major tragedies: *Hamlet, Othello, King Lear, Macbeth, Antony and Cleopatra,* and *Coriolanus*. Other Shakespearean tragedies do not belong so obviously in this grouping.

  A. The early play *Titus Andronicus* is more akin to bloody melodrama.

  B. The much loved *Romeo and Juliet* might be defined as a *tragedy of fate*, whose young protagonists are largely victims of external forces rather than adults grappling with impossible choices.

  C. The dispersed dramatic focus of *Julius Caesar* makes it more akin to a history play.

IV. Certain themes and problems regularly recur in the mature tragedies.

  A. These works explore tensions between the will and desires of the individual and the constraints emanating from his or her society—the relationship between public and private life.

  B. Shakespearean tragedies frequently anatomize the workings of power (political power, erotic power, the power of language and the imagination, the power of theater itself).

C. The major characters often question the workings of the metaphysical forces that ostensibly shape their cosmos.

D. Shakespearean tragedies are generally family matters and, therefore, much concerned with divided loyalties.

E. Shakespearean tragedies raise questions about agency: about who does or does not get to act and to reflect upon their actions in the imaginative space of these plays.

   1. They also explore the borderline between action and transgression and invite us to ponder the moments at which characters overstep a moral or social or cultural boundary.

   2. They raise questions concerning the gendering of experience and action and the seeming monopoly held by male characters on the most elevated tragic experience.

F. They regularly offer variations on the theme of *tragic knowledge*.

V. There are certain points a reader of these plays should bear in mind.

A. Shakespeare's language is challenging and complex, but he does not write in Old English. In order to deal with his astonishing vocabulary and often compressed syntax, it is important to read the plays in a good edition with detailed notes and glosses.

B. Readers should not be put off by the fact that these plays are largely written in blank verse: poetic language can render complex experience in a way that appeals both to the intellect and to the emotions.

Essential Reading:

McDonald, discussion of Shakespearean tragedy in *The Bedford Companion to Shakespeare: An Introduction with Documents*, pp. 85–90.

Supplementary Reading:

Briggs, *This Stage-Play World: Texts and Contexts, 1580–1625.*

De Grazia, "Shakespeare and the Craft of Language," in *The Cambridge Companion to Shakespeare*, Margaret de Grazia and Stanley Wells, eds.

Poole, *Tragedy: A Very Short Introduction.*

Questions to Consider:

1. Do modern plays described as tragedies seem to have the same preoccupations as Shakespearean tragedy? (You might consider such works as Arthur Miller's *Death of a Salesman* or Eugene O'Neill's *Long Day's Journey into Night.*)

2. Do you think tragic drama should be morally edifying in the ways that Philip Sidney suggests?

Lecture One—Transcript
Defining Tragedy

Let's imagine you've gone to the theater to see Shakespeare's *King Lear*. In the course of the play, you've seen an old man driven to madness by the cruelty of two of his daughters, a young man reduced to a filthy homeless beggar by the treachery of his own brother, and an old man having his eyes gouged out—onstage, no less—because his son has betrayed him to his enemies. And that's just a conservative summary of the play's horrors. At the very end of the play, the author turns the screw again. One of the villains, Edmund, has ordered the murder of Lear's loving daughter, Cordelia, almost on a whim, and Edmund's last minute repentance comes too late to save her. The old king enters, carrying his dead daughter, crazed with grief. As the other people onstage, stunned by this new atrocity, try to make sense of what is happening, Lear cradles his child and says: "No, no, no life. Why should a dog, a horse, a rat have life, And thou no breath at all? Thou'lt come no more. Never, never, never, never, never." An unanswerable question, an unspeakable grief—language to tear your very heart out. Why are you, the audience member, putting yourself through this? Why aren't you doing something more restful, like watching a rerun of *The Texas Chainsaw Massacre*?

Let me introduce myself. My name is Clare Kinney and I'm a professor of English literature at the University of Virginia. I've just given you a very small taste of one of the Shakespearian tragedies I'm going to be discussing in this course and this opening lecture will try to give you some sense of the larger issues I'll address in relation to Shakespeare's tragic drama. But, first of all, an anecdote. Some years ago I was teaching an advanced seminar on Shakespeare. My students had just read the play *As You Like It* along with a provocative essay in which a contemporary scholar offered a rather unusual interpretation of the work. We were discussing the claims of that essay when a student, a young man who was also a drama major, spoke up: "I can see that this guy is making some really smart points," he said, "but I've acted in *As You Like It*, and you know, it just didn't play like that."

I have always remembered his remark. It reminds me of two things. First, that no one account of something as rich and complex as a

Shakespeare play is ever going to contain it, is ever going to sum it up, fix its meaning, and second, that these plays aren't just texts on a page. They have a whole dimension of performance that has its own claims. Every time you see a Shakespeare play acted—whether it's by the local high school or whether it's by the Royal Shakespeare Company—you'll see, in some sense, a different version of that play.

What does this have to do with what I'm offering you? I'm certainly not trying to say that my 24 lectures aren't worth listening to. I hope to offer interpretations or mappings of these plays that will interest you and excite you. I'm going to do my darndest to make Shakespeare's language come alive for you. But, at the same time, I'm not claiming to give you the final word on the plays. I hope that in your own reading, you'll find there is room for your insights, your own discoveries, and that if you go to see any of them in performance at any time, you'll find yourself re-imagining them in yet more ways. Because, if there's one truly wonderful thing about Shakespeare, it is his capacity to keep surprising his audience. There's no "been there, done that," got the t-shirt with these plays. I'll offer you one journey through their complexities, but there will always be territory left to explore.

Since this course is about Shakespearian tragedy, we might want to start by asking, what is this 2,400-year-old fascination in the writers and audiences in the west with watching re-enactments of terrible human suffering, and, in particular, the painful experience of someone whom we label a tragic protagonist?

The earliest discussion of tragedy is to be found in Aristotle's *Poetics* around the 4th century B.C. Aristotle's account of tragedy was based on the drama of ancient Athens at that time—the work of Sophocles, Euripides, and Aeschylus, plays like *Oedipus Rex* or *Medea*. He defines tragedy as a self-contained action of a certain grandeur and scope, written in a language that is more elevated, more concentrated, than colloquial speech. Its plot will involve dramatic reversals. Shakespearian examples would be Hamlet thinking he's killed Claudius and finding he's killed Polonius. Laertes thinking he's set things up to kill Hamlet in the duel scene and being killed by his own poisoned weapon. Its protagonist will experience some kind of climactic moment of recognition or anagnorisis, and it will evoke certain emotions in the audience. Aristotle labels them pity and fear, even as it brings about the purgation—the Greek word is catharsis—

of those emotions. Its heroes are usually elevated by rank or ability over most other people without being paragons of perfect virtue, but their fall or suffering is the result of what Aristotle terms *hamartia*— an error in action—rather than pathological vice or depravity.

I'd particularly like to emphasize that it is more useful to think in terms of an error in action than to use a phrase that may be familiar to you, the tragic flaw. The tragic flaw sound bite has dogged discussions of tragedy, ever since a critic called A.C. Bradley mistranslated the Aristotelian term *hamartia*. If you discuss tragedy only in terms of the character flaws of one individual, you may ignore his or her relationship to the social forces and cultural practices of the larger world in which he or she must act. The particular crisis of a tragic protagonist is the product of an extreme combination of internal and external forces. And. it isn't always an ostensible flaw that is their undoing; in a difficult and corrupt world, they can be undone by qualities that might be considered virtues.

Aristotle speaks not only of the ideal content of tragedy, but of the effect it should have on its audience. It should evoke pity and fear. It shouldn't simply upset and disgust. It should create a kind of empathy between audience and characters and particularly between audience and tragic protagonist. There but for the grace of god go I. And his notion of catharsis suggests that the audience will be changed by the experience, will undergo some kind of purgation of the emotions that have been aroused by the play, will have their own assumptions about human experience modified by the play.

Keep thinking about this double scenario. What happens to the people in the play? What happens to us as we experience the play? Do we necessarily feel the same things as the play's protagonist? Is our vision completely continuous with his or hers? Does that character necessarily learn the same things we learn from seeing the action as a whole?

Tragedy in performance does not reappear in Europe until the 16th century. Before this, in medieval Europe, the term tragedy is often used not to describe drama, but to describe a certain kind of narrative. In Chaucer's *Canterbury Tales*, written in the late 14th century, one of Chaucer's pilgrims, the monk, relates a series of stories, which he describes as tragedies, and he defines tragedy as follows. I'm translating from the original Middle English text: "To speak of tragedy is to speak of a certain story—as old books remind us—of one who was in a position of great prosperity and who has fallen from high degree into misery and ends wretchedly." The monk's short tales involve biblical, mythological figures, as well as people from history and they suggest that, for medieval readers, tragedy is simply the story of a fall from greatness to wretchedness. This version of tragedy focuses on human beings' vulnerability to the caprices of fortune and this kind of tragedy suggests the Christian moral that one should scorn transient, earthly pleasures and glories, and trust in higher things: the rewards of virtue in the afterlife.

Let's move on a couple of hundred years. Although 16th-century writers were aware of Aristotle's ideas, their theories of tragedy were even more influenced by the plays of a Roman writer, Seneca. Some centuries after Aristotle, the Romans wrote tragic dramas in partial imitation of the Greeks, and those written by Seneca were frequently read and translated in 16th- and 17th-century England. Seneca's works are highly rhetorical, full of moral speeches, and preoccupied with death and revenge, but it is not clear whether Seneca's plays were meant for public performance or just for private reading.

When the English writer Philip Sidney defines tragedy in his *Defense of Poesy*, written around 1581, published 1595, he speaks of the:

> high and excellent Tragedy, that openeth the greatest wounds, and showeth forth the ulcers that are covered with tissue. That maketh kings fear to be tyrants. That, with stirring the effects of admiration and commiseration, teacheth the uncertainty of this world, and upon how weak foundations gilded roofs are builded.

Sidney's ideas show a mix of influences. He calls tragedy a high and excellent form. This recalls Aristotle's idea that its action must be of a special magnitude. He suggests its horrors are justified because it exposes hidden vice; it is a didactic form. It discloses the corruption that rulers and statesmen may attempt to conceal. His image is one of ulcerated skin masked by tissue, which for Sidney does not mean Kleenex, but rich cloth of any kind. Tragedy, says Sidney, makes kings fear to be tyrants. He follows the suggestion we often see in educational treatises of the Renaissance that, in mirroring nature, art can move people to virtuous action with its stirring or admonitory examples. Finally, he suggests that tragedy, in provoking admiration, which in Sidney's usage means wonder, not respect, and commiseration, "teacheth the uncertainty of this world, and upon how weak foundations gilded roofs are builded." His remark starts out with an approximation of Aristotle's theory of tragic effect. Admiration and commiseration are somewhat equivalent to terror and pity. But, he ends on a more medieval note; tragedy shows the fragility of earthly splendors. This is more like Chaucer's formula.

Now these are some of the ways in which tragedy had been defined before Shakespeare wrote his major plays. As you can see, tragedy is not a stable term. It's always being renegotiated. Later on, thinkers like Hegel and Nietzsche and Brecht will offer new definitions. And Shakespeare himself never writes a theory of tragedy, he just writes tragedies. We don't know if he ever read Aristotle or, for that matter, Sidney. Although, many commentators have, in their turn, constructed their theories of what constitutes Shakespearian tragedy. I'm going to give you a provisional list of some of the commonplaces about Shakespearian tragedy.

One: Shakespeare's tragic heroes tend to be elevated by rank and/or ability above the common herd. They are princes or warriors. Notice the gender assumptions here—the idea that the tragic protagonist is, in fact, a tragic hero, not a tragic heroine. I'll be coming back to this issue. They often exist in a state of alienation from their own society. Their experiences or the consequences of choices they have made tend to create their estrangement from ordinary human beings. Three: The fall of the tragic protagonist tends to have a larger significance. It's not just one person coming to grief, but may have reverberations within a whole community. Four: Tragic protagonists generally reach some kind of recognition of the problematic choices they have made or the destructive actions they have engaged in. They may claw out of their pain and horror a kind of insight, which allows them to find some universalizing and higher significance in their experience and suffering. This not only links their individual passions to a larger notion of the human condition, but gives us a vision of a world where significance or wonder or even a meaningful terror can be won from the chaos of life.

Finding meaning in what is horrible or fearful—this last is a particularly tempting vision for audiences at any time. The last hundred years have given us the spectacle of a world, which is still for many people, one of hideous cruelty. Think of the victims of ethnic cleansing. Think of the genocide in Rwanda. Think of 9/11 and the ongoing violence in the Middle East. Going further back, think of the victims of Hitler or Stalin or Pol Pot or the literally millions of soldiers who died in the trenches in World War I. One might well be tempted to ask, if there is a God, what kind of God could allow these horrors to happen? Come to think of that, what kind of human beings could allow these horrors to happen? Given that we seem to be stuck in a nasty, brutal, ignoble little world, it is not surprising that people have tended to value works of art, which attempt to extract some kind of meaning out of human suffering.

But, be aware that Shakespeare's contemporaries don't speak of this kind of agenda. It is later writers who have insisted that death and suffering are transcended in Renaissance tragedy because a particular vision of human nobility escapes or survives or transcends the horror of the action. These commentators would argue that the art of the tragic dramatist is to be cherished because it puts human suffering into words and makes it signify. We may wish to ask if this insight is achieved by the characters who participate in the tragic action of a particular play or whether it is retrospectively constructed by us, the audience.

Now, I've just outlined for you the commonplaces, which recur again and again in discussions of Shakespearian tragedy. I offer them as a starting point, not a tidy crystallized definition. And I invite you to test them out quite ruthlessly against our readings.

And now, a word about just what exactly we're going to be reading. This course will explore the six major tragedies Shakespeare wrote between 1600 and 1608: *Hamlet*, *Othello*, *King Lear*, *Macbeth*, *Antony and Cleopatra*, and *Coriolanus*. During this stage of his career, Shakespeare seems to focus with a particular intensity upon profound human dilemmas, upon the difficulties of enacting choice and moral agency in a corrupt world, in exploring certain experiences, which test the very limits of language. I should admit here that I am being selective in my focus. These are not the only tragedies Shakespeare wrote. We have, for example, the very early *Titus Andronicus*, the bloodiest play he ever composed, a kind of 16th-century slasher movie, and also, of course, another earlier play, the much-loved *Romeo and Juliet*. Why am I ignoring *Romeo and Juliet*? Not because it is not a fine and moving drama, but, as a tragedy, it doesn't quite fit with the works Shakespeare was to write later in his life. Its star-crossed lovers are largely the victims of forces external to themselves—the caprices of fortune and circumstance. They are very young people, who love impulsively, not adults wrestling with impossible choices or agonizing over their actions.

Another earlier tragedy, which I find difficult to put in the same box as the tragedies I'll discuss, is *Julius Caesar*. Its complicated engagement with Roman history disperses the focus of tragic attention. Caesar, its nominal protagonist, dies in Act 2. The dilemmas of Brutus, his deeply ethical assassin, get a fair bit of attention, but must share center stage with the machinations of Cassius and with the political maneuvering of Mark Antony and Octavius. The historical vision it offers is shot through with tragedy, but not defined by tragedy. Furthermore, even as it ends, the seeds of a new conflict are germinating between the victorious survivors. Shakespeare will return to the aftermath of this play to write a work in which, I shall argue, tragedy rather more conclusively stakes its own claims over history. That play, which we'll be exploring later in this course, is *Antony and Cleopatra*.

So, let me offer a brief summary of what we'll be looking at in the plays written between 1600 and 1608. In considering the very particular universes Shakespeare creates, I'll be stressing the importance of state and social politics in these plays. Tensions they explore between the will and desires of the individual and the constraints emanating from his or her society, the relationship between public and private life. Shakespearian tragedy involves complicated negotiations of power and we'll consider the different kinds of power under investigation: political power, erotic power, the power of language and the imagination, the power of theater itself. "The play's the thing wherein I'll catch the conscience of the king." There's also the little matter of the ways in which Shakespeare's characters imagine powers beyond humanity. Is there providence in the fall of a sparrow, as Hamlet declares, or do the gods kill us for their sport, as the Earl of Gloucester despairingly remarks in King Lear?

Shakespearian tragedies are family matters and I'll be thinking about the pressures of kinship. Protagonists are differently positioned in the familial structure. Hamlet and Coriolanus are defined primarily as sons; Macbeth and Othello as husbands; King Lear as a father, and the tragedies of *Hamlet*, *Othello*, and *Lear* offer us some telling accounts of father/daughter relations.

I'll have a lot to say about agency, about who does or does not get to act and to reflect upon their actions in the imaginative space of these plays, and I'll be looking in great detail at the fine borderline between action and transgression. We might indeed think of transgression as being coterminous with tragic action. What constitutes transgression in these plays, what does it mean in different worlds and different contexts to overstep the boundaries of permitted action, to challenge the norms of one's society, to put oneself beyond the pale? Why do we find that moment so compelling?

This may be linked to questions concerning gendered action in the plays. The four major tragedies go by the names of their heroes— Hamlet, Othello, Lear, and Macbeth. Cleopatra shares double billing with Antony. Can women be tragic heroines? Can their experience be represented as tragic? This will oblige us to investigate what constitutes or defines the kind of action we call tragedy. If women aren't usually the tragic protagonists, what do we make of the fact that their actions—or what are perceived as their transgressions— often seem to trigger the tragic action: Gertrude's marriage to her dead husband's brother in *Hamlet*; Desdemona's elopement with an alien general in *Othello*; Lady Macbeth's spurring Macbeth on to murder; Cordelia refusing to play her father's game at the start of *King Lear*? Finally, we'll consider that whole business of tragic knowledge and insight won out of suffering that I've mentioned before. What kind of significance do Shakespeare's protagonists find in their own suffering?

These are some of the main issues I'll be addressing, but to conclude, a few words about the business of reading Shakespeare. From time to time, my own English majors come and sort of whine to me a bit about the difficulty of Shakespeare's Old English. This is Old English: "Hwaet, we gardena in geardagum Theodcyninga thrym gefrunon." That's the beginning of Beowulf; it's not what Shakespeare writes. Then, we have Middle English: "Whan that Aprille with his shoures soote / The droghte of Marche hath perced to the roote." That's the very beginning of Chaucer's *Canterbury Tales*. It's not what Shakespeare writes.

Let me just give you a little taste of what Shakespeare does write and invite you as I pronounce what is officially Modern English. Just listen and note mentally any words of which you don't recognize the meaning.

> "Tomorrow and tomorrow and tomorrow creeps in this petty pace from day to day to the last syllable of recorded time. And all our yesterdays have guided fools the way to dusty death. Out, out, brief candle. Life's but a walking shadow. A poor player that struts and frets his hour upon the stage and then is heard no more. It is a tale told by an idiot full of sound and fury, signifying nothing."

That soliloquy of Macbeth's, in fact, doesn't contain a single word that isn't in common use today. Now, I did cheat a bit. We have to admit that Shakespeare uses some words, which are now archaic or whose nuances have shifted somewhat. He also has a vocabulary about three times as large as the most articulate of us. The lexicon of his complete works is about 25,000 words. His syntax is occasionally more compressed or elliptical than ours. He is very culturally literate and his range of illusion is daunting, which is why it's important that you read a good edition with glosses and footnotes. Shakespeare also, of course, writes plays, which are largely, although by no means wholly, written in poetry, in blank verse—unrhymed verse in the five beat lines we call iambic pentameter.

Many people have what I call fear of poetry. My own English majors will say things like, I really love literature except that I don't like poetry. Poetic seems to mean, for these people, extra words, hidden meanings, superfluous ornament, frills, static—things that make life difficult for the 21st-century reader. My definition of poetic language is rather different. It's language under pressure, often bound by certain patterns or rhythms, which don't hamper communication so much as discipline it. Shakespeare's poetic language, I'd maintain, is one whose apparent ornaments and superfluities can actually offer the most economic, most precise way of saying something or conveying a complex effect that appeals both to the intellect and to the emotions. Macbeth could have said life's a bitch and then we die. But, his poor player, his tale told by an idiot, is a far more suggestive way of conveying what he wants to say about existence.

One final piece of advice: As you read the plays, remember that play texts are not like poems or novels. They have the extra dimension of performance, which allows directors and actors to make interventions in the text, to reinterpret it and represent it in different ways. I'll be addressing performance issues from time to time in my lectures, but you should also keep thinking about the problems and possibilities opened up by performance. The different ways a scene might be played. The way the literal embodiment of the action can inflect meaning.

I've talked in this lecture about how we might define tragedy and what seem to be some of the particular preoccupations of Shakespearian tragedy. I have not yet addressed the very specific historical context in which Shakespeare was writing his plays. My second lecture will focus upon the experiments in writing tragic drama that were taking place in the late 16th century when Shakespeare's career began and that offered him his own literary springboards. I'll also glance at the social and political history of the early 17th century when the major tragedies were written, both the big issues of the day and the more everyday preoccupations of Shakespeare's audience. Shakespeare's tragedies often unfold in geographically distant places or are set in a far off past, but they are often shaped and inflected by matters surprisingly close to home, but more on that subject next time.

Lecture Two
Shakespearean Tragedy in Context

Scope:

After a concise introduction to performance conditions and attitudes toward the theater in Shakespeare's England, this lecture will explore two different contexts for thinking about Shakespearean tragedy. It first offers an overview of some of the tragic drama written for the Elizabethan stage prior to Shakespeare's composition of *Hamlet*, paying particular attention to the innovations of Christopher Marlowe in such plays as *Tamburlaine* and *Doctor Faustus* and to Thomas Kyd's highly influential treatment of revenge in *The Spanish Tragedy*. It then offers some remarks on the reign of King James I (during which all but one of Shakespeare's major tragedies were written). The tragedies written by Shakespeare and his contemporaries feature many corrupt power brokers, and the characters who populate these plays have little confidence that their universe is controlled by benign metaphysical forces. Such works seem to speak to the preoccupations and anxieties of the playwright's own historical moment.

Outline

I. Shakespeare's tragedies were acted in an era when performance conditions (and attitudes toward theater as an art form) differed significantly from those of our own day.

    A. Shakespeare wrote at the very beginning of the invention of the English theater as we know it; the first permanent theaters were built from 1576 onward outside the official boundaries of the city of London.

    B. Theaters aroused criticism from their very inception.

        1. They were places that encouraged the mingling of different classes and where the players challenged notions of "natural" hierarchy by impersonating kings and nobles.

        2. Women's parts were played by young boys until the late 17th century, and critics were suspicious of the blurring of gender distinctions this produced.

3. The works we now consider high art were viewed by some of Shakespeare's contemporaries as popular entertainment at best and a source of social and moral corruption at worst. Philip Stubbes's *Anatomy of Abuses* (1583) offers a particularly sustained and virulent denunciation of the London stage.

C. Plays were acted in the afternoons by natural light in the public theaters; the private, enclosed playhouses attracted a wealthier clientele.

D. A large part of London's population attended the theater regularly, and companies had very large repertories.

II. Before Shakespeare wrote his major tragedies, there had already been some significant recent experiments in this genre.

A. Thomas Sackville's and Thomas Norton's *Gorboduc* is written in imitation of the Latin plays of Seneca and creates a precedent for the writing of political tragedy; its plot about the unhappy consequences of the division of a kingdom anticipates that of *King Lear*.

B. Christopher Marlowe's *Tamburlaine* and *Doctor Faustus* are particularly striking and influential Elizabethan tragedies.

1. Marlowe creates protagonists who characteristically set their will in opposition to existing norms and hierarchies.

2. Even when orthodox morality is reasserted, as in the fall of Faustus, the aesthetic interest of the play tends to lie in the speeches of the tragic protagonist.

3. Marlowe's brilliant deployment of poetic language sets a precedent for what might be achieved with English blank verse; Shakespeare builds upon his linguistic experiments.

C. Thomas Kyd's *The Spanish Tragedy* started a fashion for revenge tragedies.

1. The heroes of revenge tragedies attempt to enforce justice by their own actions in a world in which public and political institutions are corrupt.

2. Revenge tragedies deploy graphic on-stage violence, and the destruction of evil also involves much slaughter of

the innocent.

    3. The plot of *The Spanish Tragedy* anticipates that of *Hamlet*; its protagonist feigns lunacy, and it features a striking play within the play that the hero uses for his own purposes.

III. Shakespeare wrote nearly all of his tragedies during the reign of James I of England; his plays are, to some extent, shaped by his historical moment.

    A. Both Shakespearean and non-Shakespearean Jacobean tragedy is often concerned with corruption in high places and the destructive effects of power; in this, it seems to echo particular anxieties of the period.

    B. James I clashed regularly with Parliament over questions of royal prerogative; his court was perceived as being significantly more lax and debauched than that of his predecessor, Elizabeth I.

    C. Social and economic problems (such as galloping inflation) increased during James's reign.

    D. An expanded access to education among men of lower rank threw into clearer light the limits of the autocratic political system.

    E. The notion that worldly existence was merely the gateway to the higher reality of the afterlife had been attenuated by a new secularism and skepticism.

IV. The tragedies of this period tend to have multiple agendas.

    A. Their authors may not only consider the painful experiences of an individual in spiritual or metaphysical terms but also interrogate the manmade forces and structures that promote inhumane behavior.

    B. Metaphysical questions tend to get transformed into political questions. Revenge tragedies may encourage their audiences to ask what sociopolitical circumstances and forces might provoke an individual to act outside the law and to ignore the strictures of religion.

Essential Reading:

McDonald, "Performances, Playhouses and Players," in *The Bedford Companion to Shakespeare: An Introduction with Documents*, pp. 109–127.

Supplementary Reading:

Kerrigan, *Revenge Tragedy: Aeschylus to Armageddon*, chapter 1.

Kyd, *The Spanish Tragedy*.

Lockyer, *James VI and I*, chapter 4.

Marlowe, *Tamburlaine* and *Doctor Faustus*.

Questions to Consider:

1. In what ways might the new skepticism in religious and philosophical thought evident in the late 16th and early 17th centuries have fostered the writing of tragedy?

2. Revenge plots are still popular in contemporary plays, novels, and films. How might their presentation in our own culture differ from their treatment in the drama of Shakespeare's day?

Lecture Two—Transcript
Shakespearean Tragedy in Context

In this lecture, I'd like to offer a few historical contexts for thinking about Shakespearean tragedy. I shall first offer some background about the performance conditions and attitudes towards theatrical performance in late 16th- and early 17th-century England when Shakespeare wrote his plays. I shall then go on to discuss some of the tragedies that were being written for the Elizabethan stage a little before Shakespeare's composition of *Hamlet*. And finally, I shall offer some remarks on the reign of King James I, who ruled from 1603 to 1625, the period in which all but one of Shakespeare's major tragedies were written. I shall suggest how the playwright's work might speak to the preoccupations and anxieties of his own historical moment.

Shakespeare lived from 1564–1616. His plays were written roughly between 1590 and 1613. He writes at the very beginning of the invention of the English theater as we know it. That is, when plays are first being written in large numbers as secular and commercial entertainment. In 1576, James Burbage builds the first permanent theater building in England. The 1580s and 1590s saw the construction of several more. In 1598, the Globe Theatre was built and eventually became the permanent home of Shakespeare's company. All the theaters were built outside what were then the official administrative boundaries of the city of London. This was not a high-class area. It was full of the kind of places that wanted to be beyond the limits of the city ordinances—the brothels, and the pits for bear and bull baiting and cock fights. All the kinds of places that annoyed the good solid merchants because they drew their apprentices and workpeople away from the business of the day.

Theatres were from the start a cause of controversy and contention. They were places where the divisions of a society, which was much more hierarchical than ours, were put in question. Nobles, trades people, and the roughest laborers rubbed shoulders in the audience. Playacting itself challenged notions of hierarchy. Players, actors, didn't fit in with the class system, but were, in fact, dangerously adept at impersonating all kinds of people. These people, these actors, these people of dubious status could imitate kings and lords and generals, and they thus, by their very actions, challenged the notion that nobility or courage was something inherent or inherited and mainly or indeed only to be associated with high birth. These people could perform nobility. The stage was also a place where gender distinctions became blurred. In England, until the late 17th century, there were no professional actresses. Young boys played all the women's roles.

All of these things provoked several writers to denounce the whole phenomenon of the popular theater. What we now think of as high art was seen by a fair number of Shakespeare's contemporaries as a source of social and moral corruption. Philip Stubbes, a radical Protestant critic of the stage, wrote a lengthy treatise called *The Anatomy of Abuses* in 1583. In it, he denounced the theaters and all those who acted in them. Stubbes is particularly paranoid about men playing women's parts. He writes: "Our apparel was given us as a sign distinctive to discern between sex and sex, and therefore one to wear the apparel of another sex is to participate with the same and to adulterate the verities of his own kind." Men playing women, he argues, might as well "be called hermaphrodites, monsters of both kinds, half women, half men."

Originally, theaters were more like amphitheaters. They were open to the sky and had no artificial lighting. Plays were performed in the afternoons. A stage thrust out into the middle of the theater building, which was usually polygonal in shape. The audience either stood in the pit in front of and around the stage, or if they paid more, could sit in the galleries on the sides of the building. Later, we get the private indoor theaters. These are much more expensive to attend. A particular famous one of these was the Blackfriars Theatre, which would eventually be used by Shakespeare's own company, The King's Men, and, in fact, not very far from where I teach at the University of Virginia in Charlottesville, just over the mountains in Stanton, there is a wonderful reconstruction of the Blackfriars Theatre. One important thing to bear in mind is that a person doesn't have to be literate in order to be able to understand and enjoy the action of a play. So, it isn't just the educated people who were found at the open-air theaters.

The theater companies played every day, except the major church holidays. Well, they couldn't play in bad weather, of course and the theaters were closed during times of plague epidemic for fear that people massed together would help spread contagion, and plague epidemics are a reality at this time. There were violent outbreaks of

Bubonic Plague in 1592, 1594, and 1603, which closed the theaters. The companies had very large repertories; plays were learned, rehearsed, and performed in swift succession, and 10 days would be a very long run for a new play. London, at this time, has a population of about 200,000 people, and surviving records from the Globe Theatre indicate that that theater was able to hold about 3,000 people. And people went to theater a lot, so a fast turnover of plays was needed. We know, again from surviving records, that in the season of 1594 to 1595, the company known as the Lord Admiral's Men performed 38 plays, 21 of them newly written, which means a new play would have been added every two weeks or so.

Plays weren't thought to belong to high culture, to literature at all. Many hundreds of them were churned out between the 1580s and 1642. After 1642, the theaters were closed for almost two decades as a result of the more puritanical parliamentarians coming to power in the English Civil War. To be a playwright was not an elevated profession; it wasn't initially perceived as being an artist. Indeed, when the poet Ben Jonson, who also wrote plays, published his complete works in the early 17th century, many of his readers were amazed that he included his plays among them, as if they were the same kind of artistic objects as his lyric poetry. Shakespeare's work, which we tend to oh so respectfully as monumentally High Culture, with capital letters, was originally part of the popular culture of his time—entertainment for ordinary, even sub-literate folks.

As I mentioned in my previous lecture, Shakespeare writes his major tragedies between 1600 and 1608. But, let's first look at some of the tragedies produced by other playwrights between 1558, when Queen Elizabeth I came to the throne, and the writing of *Hamlet* in 1601— the forerunners, as it were, of Shakespearean tragedy.

In 1562, Thomas Sackville and Thomas Norton write *Gorboduc*. This play was written before even the first permanent theater was built by Burbage, but we do have evidence that it was performed at court before Queen Elizabeth. We can see in it certain features that we take for granted in Shakespearean drama, but which were new at the time. It has a five-act structure, a design which is derived from the classical Latin plays of the Roman author Seneca, who was much admired by Shakespeare's contemporaries and it's written in blank verse—that is, in the unrhymed verse lines in the particular rhythm we call iambic pentameter.

Iambic pentameter is a fancy way of saying that the line consists of five groups of two syllables in which the poetic stress is put on the second syllable. The sound is basically dedum dedum dedum dedum dedum. "Thou knowst the mask of night is on my face," says Juliet to Romeo, in perfect iambic pentameter. Now, it would be really boring if every single line in a verse drama had that precise rhythm. It functions as a kind of template on which rhythmical variations are made. At any rate, this is the verse form in which Shakespeare writes the greater part of his tragedies and I'll have a little more to say about it later.

But, going back to Sackville and Norton's play *Gorboduc*. *Gorboduc* is a political tragedy set in ancient Britain. It concerns the unhappy results of King Gorboduc's ignoring his counselor's advice and deciding to divide his kingdom between his two sons, an act which results in his own death, and also in the murder of one brother by the other, civil war, and a whole scale rebellion of the nobility. It sounds pretty exciting, but as all the physical action occurs offstage and is reported by messengers, and as the play is written in really, really boring verse, it is not. However, it does create a precedent in English drama for the writing of political tragedy and it shows that Elizabethan playwrights were interested from the very start in such questions as the proper actions of a king, the limits of his powers, and the conflict between the will of the individual and the duty he owes to his state. Shakespeare himself will write a tragic drama centered upon the unhappy consequences of the division of a kingdom. He'll call it *King Lear*.

Now, in 1588, we have a huge popular hit in the form of two plays: *Tamburlaine* and its sequel, *Tamburlaine Part 2*, by Christopher Marlowe. Marlowe, who is an exact contemporary of Shakespeare's—they were born the same year, 1564—was a brilliant, unorthodox, highly gifted writer who came to an untimely end in a tavern brawl at the age of 30. In the interim, he had almost certainly been employed as a spy by Queen Elizabeth's ministers, and historians have theorized that his ostensibly accidental death may actually have been a political assassination. Marlowe, in fact, was already in trouble at the time of his death for his alleged atheism and for his radical opinions and for his tendency to make such rash public statements as, "All they that love not tobacco and boys are fools." If you've ever seen the movie *Shakespeare in Love*, you may have seen a rather splendid bravura performance by Rupert Everett as Christopher Marlowe.

Marlowe's *Tamburlaine* presents the rise to power of a hero of humble origin, a shepherd who ends up conquering most of Asia Minor. His campaigns are carried out with great brutality, and the blood and guts are not banished offstage. The play is full of spectacle, climaxing when Tamburlaine enters in triumph in a chariot pulled by the kings he has conquered and whipping them on, calling them pampered jades of Asia. Tamburlaine takes his destiny in his own hands, claims a godlike power to enforce his will upon the world. He says, "I hold the fates bound fast in iron chains. And with my hand turn Fortune's wheel about." Although the limits of his will become clear at the end of *Tamburlaine Part 2* when he faces his own mortality, the plays give more room to his rise than his fall. They thus challenge, to some extent, the medieval notion of tragedy as being largely focused upon the fall of people from high places. Nor is it Tamburlaine's pride which destroys or limits him at the end, so much as the simple fact that he's mortal, subject to time—that he's not immune to death.

In a later play, *Doctor Faustus,* 1592, Marlowe again shows us a low-born individual setting up his will against all norms and hierarchies, a man who wishes to fashion himself according to his own desires. Tamburlaine challenged the pagan fates. Faustus challenges the Christian world order and God himself. Faustus is a scholar who is frustrated by the notion of any kind of limit, including the limits of his own humanity. He has excelled in all intellectual disciplines. "Yet art thou still but Faustus and a man," he laments and commits the ultimate transgression of selling his soul to Satan for superhuman powers and knowledge. But, he can't escape the limits of his humanity. Indeed, in his final speech, spoken as the minutes tick relentlessly away from the last hour before the devil will claim him and he will be damned forever, he begs God to let him enter again a system of limitations. "Impose some end on my incessant pain. Let Faustus live in hell a thousand years, a hundred thousand and at last be saved."

After Faustus has been torn to pieces by devils, the play's chorus offers us a more conventional moral, which points to the errors of human overreaching, the destructiveness of humanity transgressing its proper limits. "Faustus is gone, regard his hellish fall, whose fiendful fortune may exhort the wise only to wonder at unlawful things." But, this concluding reassertion of orthodox morality remains in tension with the more powerful and evocative language of the aspiring and suffering Faustus. In the last hour of his life, for example, as he waits for the devil to come and drag him to hell, Faustus's agony is articulated in astonishing poetry. Even before he is literally in hell, his language offers us proof that hell is a state of mind, and it might be that, because of the resonance of his speeches, Marlowe's protagonist triumphs poetically, if not morally. The kind of challenge his desires offer to the status quo aren't completely defused or recontained by the final moralizing commentary of the chorus.

In both *Tamburlaine* and *Doctor Faustus*, a significant amount of the heroic action lies in the hero's language. Marlowe's often singled out for showing just what can be done with the blank verse line. Indeed, Marlowe's brilliant manipulation of the flexible rhythms of iambic pentameter, far more coruscating than the drab verse of *Gorboduc*, sets a fashion that prevailed for the next 50 years among English playwrights. Shakespeare would build upon Marlowe's experiments in blank verse.

Now, just to let you hear the way Marlowe's contemporaries had been writing verse drama, here's an excerpt from a play called *Cambyses* written by Thomas Preston in 1561 about a tyrannical Persian ruler. The hero-villain has just received his death wound:

> "Out, alas! What shall I do? My life is finished. Wounded I am by sudden chance, my blood is minished. I feel myself a-dying now; of life bereft am I. And Death hath caught me with his dart; for want of blood I spy [expire]. Thus gasping here on ground I lie; for nothing do I care. A just reward for my misdeeds my death doth plain declare."

As you can hear, it's horrible, clunky bombast, and it's written in a rather unfortunate seven-beat line that lends itself to poetic anticlimax. Here, by contrast, is Marlowe's *Doctor Faustus*, greeting the famous beauty, Helen of Troy, who has been summoned by the devil to satisfy his desires, dreaming of the power that magic may offer him:

> "Was this the face that launched a thousand ships and burnt the topless towers of Ilium? Sweet Helen, make me immortal

with a kiss. Her lips suck forth my soul, see where it flies. Come Helen come, give me my soul again. Here will I dwell, for heaven be in these lips, and all is dross that is not Helena."

Marlowe's blank verse captures the flexible rhythms of ordinary speech, even as it gives it a formal ordering that exploits the poetic possibilities of language.

Another popular, influential play of the late 16th century was *The Spanish Tragedy* by Thomas Kyd, 1587. It starts a fashion for what we call revenge tragedies—plays which show individuals trying to enforce justice by their own actions in a world whose public and political institutions are corrupt. The hero is Hieronimo, whose son is assassinated by some highborn villains. After plunging into madness, he emerges from it to devise a plan in which, undercover of presenting a theatrical entertainment, he will turn mock deaths into real ones and kill off his enemies. When this succeeds and the stage is littered with corpses, he bites off his tongue so he can't be interrogated. Every act of violence, including the tongue chewing-off, takes place onstage, in contrast to *Gorboduc* and also to the tragedies of classical antiquity, where death and destruction were always reported by messengers. Hieronimo's one-man campaign against evil takes down most of the good characters as well; everyone is infected by the corruption of the court. A character desperate for revenge and on the verge of madness uses theater for his own purposes and brings a train of destruction in his wake. Does this remind you of anything? It has often been suggested that Kyd's play influenced Shakespeare's composition of *Hamlet*.

I've tried to suggest some of the concerns, some of the master plots for tragedy already popular by the time Shakespeare writes *Hamlet*. We should also note the actual historical context in which Shakespeare writes his tragedies. Queen Elizabeth I of England died in 1603. All the major tragedies, except *Hamlet*, appeared after her death. Elizabeth had never married. She had wanted her own independence and that of her country, had cleverly insisted she was married to England alone, and she was succeeded by James I, her second cousin, who was already King James VI of Scotland and would rule as James I of England from 1603–1625. So, we've moved from the Elizabethan world to what historians call the Jacobean period, just as Shakespeare himself turns from the comedies and histories of his earlier career to writing his chief tragedies. Jacobean is a word that is simply derived from the Latin word for James, Jacobus.

Both Shakespearian and non-Shakespearian Jacobean tragedy is very dark indeed, preoccupied with the notion of corruption in high places and the destructive effects of power. Shakespeare's major tragedies are set in spaces that are geographically distant or in the far off past, whether they are in contemporary Venice and Cyprus, or pre-Christian Britain, or 11th-century Scotland, or ancient Rome. But, wherever and whenever they unfold, they may well gesture towards contemporary British preoccupations and anxieties.

To some extent, the plays of this time seem to reflect the changes in England between two reigns. Elizabeth I was a successful and popular monarch, although her reign was darkened at the end when the unmarried and childless queen neared her death and refused until the very last moment to designate her successor, which created a good deal of anxiety and fear that her demise would be followed by a political crisis. It may not be coincidental that *Hamlet*, written at the very end of her reign, is very much concerned with issues of inheritance, of succession, and of with the passing on of the kingdom.

James I was not a popular king and his reign saw a series of clashes between the monarch and the parliament, which would eventually climax, a generation after his death, in the English Civil War. The new king was much less skilled in manipulating the nobles and parliament than Elizabeth had been. He insisted on the absolute power of the monarch, the divine right of kings, while being less than sensitive to the moral obligation of kings. His court was significantly more corrupt than Elizabeth's and he conspicuously promoted the interest of his own favorite courtiers. He sold off public offices and sold off trade monopolies. He even sold off knighthoods quite blatantly. Meanwhile, England was suffering from galloping inflation, and while education was spreading to the middle classes, there was little sense of a meritocracy where the educated offspring of non-noble families could get a foothold in public life, or could get public office. There was a lot of unrewarded ability around, a lot of educated discontent.

The expansions of the Renaissance, the broader circulation of learning, the expanded geography disclosed by the voyages of discovery, even new possibilities for high living and refined existence, all these only threw into clearer light the limits of the autocratic political system, as well as other metaphysical limits. This is still a world of easy death. Many women die young from childbirth and many other people die young from disease. Plague epidemics, I've already mentioned, are regular. The medieval notion that this life is merely the gateway to the higher reality of the afterlife had been attenuated by a new secularism, a new interest in individual human action in the here and now. But, if this life was all there might be, then its limitations and uncertainties were, for many able men, all the more dispiriting.

Which brings us back to the notion of tragedy as a mode in which the problems of evil and injustice and the mysteries of the human condition, in general, could be reexamined—where one might try to find significance in suffering and put it in some larger pattern. At the same time, the writer of tragic drama might not only raise questions about how to make sense of the sufferings of the individual in spiritual or metaphysical terms. He might also ask questions about what we should make of the man-made forces and structures, which promote people's inhumanity to one another.

Renaissance tragedy shows a good deal of interest in the inadequacy of human institutions to enforce justice. Some of these plays hammer away at the manner in which public structures seem to come into conflict with the desires or happiness of the individual. They explore the hypocrisies, which blind whole societies to the discrepancies between the ways they profess to live and their actual actions.

To put it another way, the metaphysical questions tragedy takes up, such as, what is the morality of individual revenge, have an interesting tendency to turn into political questions. If a society's laws forbid murder, if a society's religion insists that vengeance belongs to God and not to man and that thou shalt not kill, what are the forces at work within such a society that could bring someone to feel that acting outside the law and ignoring the structures of religious belief is not only a moral obligation, but the only possible course of action?

Which brings us, of course, to *Hamlet*. But, a word before we start actually exploring this play: I'm hoping that you will read the plays yourselves before you listen to my lectures. You'll get far more out of my presentations that way. Some of you may have studied some of these plays in high school or elsewhere. I would like you to start your readings by trying to clear your head of all preconceptions you may have about them. Read like a virgin. Rediscover them. These works are infinitely susceptible to re-reading. I've been finding out new things about them for decades. I won't, incidentally, be offering you nice, tidy interpretations of them; I will be much more interested in laying out their complexities, raising lots of questions about them, and leaving space for you to ponder them further—and now, onward to *Hamlet*!

Lecture Three
Hamlet I—"Stand and unfold yourself"

Scope:

Hamlet begins with a sentry's command to "Stand and unfold [identify, disclose] yourself." This lecture addresses the work's fascination with secrets, with disclosure—and with things that cannot be put into words. It will discuss Hamlet's own "self-unfolding" in his first soliloquy; the first two acts' "unfolding" of the multiple family dramas that introduce us to the hero's foils, Fortinbras and Laertes; and the "unfolding" of the Ghost's terrible secret history to the prince.

The Ghost presents Hamlet with the impossible command to avenge his father without tainting his mind in the process. A concluding meditation on the play's emphasis on the power of memory will address Shakespeare's interest in anatomizing parent/child relations in a world in which a father can seek to control his son's actions even from beyond the grave.

Outline

I. The sentry's command to "Stand and unfold yourself" in the first scene of *Hamlet* offers a suggestive point of entry into the play.

   A. To "unfold yourself" means to disclose your identity but also to tell your story.

   B. The last thing Hamlet will do before he dies is ask Horatio to relate his story properly to those who survive him.

   C. The play is full of people demanding that other people "unfold themselves," and the Ghost wishes to "unfold" to Hamlet the story of his murder.

II. At the same time, the play is pervaded by a sense of things untold and untellable.

   A. Hamlet insists he has grief within him that "passes show."

   B. The Ghost suggests that he could tell Hamlet horrors about the afterlife that he is withholding.

   C. We ourselves might ask whether the mysteries of this play can ever be fully unfolded.

III. The play's beginning also offers some unfolding of recent political history.

    A. We learn from Horatio about "young Fortinbras," nephew of the king of Norway, and his desire to avenge his father (killed by Hamlet's father).

    B. Fortinbras, although hardly ever on stage, becomes a foil or double for "young Hamlet," who has also lost his father.

    C. Neither Fortinbras nor Hamlet seems to have automatically succeeded his father to the throne: Denmark is an "elective" monarchy.

IV. The second scene of *Hamlet* discloses the anxieties and resentments underpinning the relations between Hamlet and his mother and stepfather.

    A. Claudius attempts to play substitute father to Hamlet while keeping him under surveillance.

    B. Gertrude criticizes the extremity of Hamlet's mourning for his father and is criticized in her turn for implying that he is merely "acting out" his grief.

    C. Hamlet's first soliloquy reveals the deeper reasons behind his alienation and world-weariness.

        1. We see his horror at his mother's speedy (and, technically, incestuous) remarriage to his uncle.

        2. He makes clear his personal loathing for Claudius.

        3. He perceives his mother's sexuality as a kind of animal lust.

        4. But his emotional energy is entirely focused on the marriage of Gertrude and Claudius; he shows no resentment that he is not king.

V. Our introduction to Polonius and his children offers another scene in which family and political relations converge and a woman's actions provoke anxiety.

    A. Laertes and Polonius, like Hamlet, want to "police" the sexuality of a kinswoman; they assume that Hamlet's intentions toward Ophelia may be dishonorable.

B. Polonius's unfeeling treatment of Ophelia suggests that he is mainly interested in the market value of her virginity.

C. Although Hamlet may walk "with a larger tether" than Ophelia is permitted, it seems that the older generations seek to control the actions of *all* the younger people in this play.

VI. The earlier scenes between parents and children climax in Hamlet's encounter with his father's ghost.

A. The status of the Ghost is complicated by its references to purgatory (whose existence was denied by English Protestant doctrine).

B. Both the presence of the Ghost and the tale it tells expand upon Marcellus's remark that "something is rotten in the state of Denmark."

C. The Ghost's "unfolding" of the murder done by Claudius pours metaphorical poison in Hamlet's ear, just as Claudius poured poison in the living King Hamlet's ear.

D. The Ghost's specific command that, in avenging his father, Hamlet neither "taint" his mind nor act against his mother places the prince in an impossible position.

  1. Hamlet's mind has already been "tainted" by the Ghost's history.

  2. Hamlet remains obsessed with Gertrude's actions.

E. The Ghost's command to "remember me" leads Hamlet to imagine erasing his previous identity and subordinating his soul to the commands of his dead father.

F. Hamlet's overwhelming revulsion at what he must do may arise from the fact that despite his distaste for merely "seeming," he must now mask and dissimulate his horrible knowledge.

Essential Reading:

Shakespeare, *Hamlet.*

Supplementary Reading:

Greenblatt, *Hamlet in Purgatory*, chapter 5.

Questions to Consider:

1. Polonius's speech of advice to Laertes is well known and often quoted. How might our attitude toward Polonius's apparently sage counsel be complicated by the scene at the start of Act 2, in which he sends his servant Reynaldo to spy upon his son?

2. Just before the Ghost materializes in 1.4., Hamlet ponders the Danish national character and moves on to some larger philosophical observations. Why might Shakespeare have chosen to give him this speech at this particular moment in the play?

Lecture Three—Transcript
Hamlet I—"Stand and unfold yourself"

Beginnings are always important and Shakespeare is particularly skilled at quietly planting the seeds of later developments, as well as creating a certain mood or tone through his use of language within the first few scenes of his plays. I'm going to start my discussion of *Hamlet* by looking at the very first words of Act 1, scene 1. We're on the ramparts of the castle of Elsinore with two edgy sentries. We can tell they're edgy because the relieving sentry, Bernardo, challenges Francisco, the man already on guard, instead of the other way round. "Who's there?" says Bernardo and Francisco replies, "Nay, answer me. Stand and unfold yourself." Unfold yourself—it means to disclose your identity, but also, to tell your story. Later on, when Hamlet encounters his father's ghost, the spirit commands him to "lend thy serious hearing to what I shall unfold."

I'd like to emphasize the importance of unfolding in this play. In fact, the last thing its hero will do as he dies is to ask his friend Horatio to relate, to unfold his story properly to those who survive him. Act 1 is full of demands for people to unfold themselves or to unfold information. The soldier Marcellus wants to know why Denmark is in a state of military alert. Queen Gertrude wants to know why Hamlet persists in mourning his father, refuses to temper his grief. Ophelia's father, Polonius, wants to know what exactly has been going on between her and Hamlet. Everyone who sees the ghost asks it to tell them what it is and what it wants. Horatio later wants Hamlet to tell him and Marcellus what the ghost had to say for itself, and the ghost, of course, wishes to unfold to Hamlet just what it is that is rotten in the state of Denmark.

But, all these requests to unfold are accompanied from the start by a sense of things untold and untellable. Well before the ghost's appearance fills the sentries on the ramparts with foreboding, just as Bernardo takes over sentry duty from Francisco, Francisco says, "For this relief much thanks. 'Tis bitter cold and I am sick at heart." We're not going to see any more of Francisco and we don't know why he is sick at heart, but his words point to a malaise that hovers over everybody in the play. And, of course, we'll soon be meeting somebody else who's sick at heart—Hamlet, who insists that he has grief within him that "passes show," that can't really be made fully and authentically public. Secrets abound. A few scenes later, the ghost will tell Hamlet that if he were to relate the secrets of his experience in the afterlife, he "could a tale unfold whose lightest word would harrow up thy soul," would horrify his son's soul, and then proceeds not to tell that tale. So, we must also ask, can the secrets of this play ever be fully unfolded?

What the first scene does offer is some unfolding of recent political history. We learn from Horatio that Denmark is full of war preparations because of a previous war in which the dead King Hamlet defeated and killed Fortinbras, king of Norway, and won a portion of his lands from him. Now, young Fortinbras, Norway's son, who is bold and reckless—he's described as hot and full—is mustering an army, intent on avenging his father and winning the territory back by force. It's interesting that young Fortinbras is invoked here, because the same phrasing is used to describe Prince Hamlet himself when he's mentioned for the first time. Horatio says, "Let us impart what we have seen tonight, unto young Hamlet." Young Fortinbras, young Hamlet—both of them young men with dead fathers.

Fortinbras only actually appears on stage twice in the whole play, and he and Hamlet never exchange a word, but he's a lurking off-stage presence, and as another son with a motive for revenge, a sort of double to Hamlet. We will see King Claudius sending ambassadors to the current king of Norway, whom we learn is Fortinbras's uncle, telling him to clamp down on Fortinbras's military ambitions. So, Fortinbras, like Hamlet, is the son of a dead king, a young man whose uncle has succeeded his father to the throne. You'll notice, incidentally, that nobody in Denmark is going around saying, why isn't young Hamlet king? The medieval chronicle history from which the plot of this play ultimately derives concerns a Denmark in the very distant past. At that time, Denmark was an elective monarchy and the son of the preceding monarch didn't necessarily inherit the throne. Nonetheless, Claudius's current actions are dubious, in so far as he's also married his dead brother's wife, which in Shakespeare's time was technically an incestuous marriage.

Act 1, scene 2 slides from state politics into family dynamics and, in particular, parents seeking to control and contain the behavior of children. Of course, we're still really in political territory. In Denmark, the personal is the political. After sending his ambassadors to Norway, Claudius's next order of business is with two young men who want to leave town. He cheerfully permits Laertes, the son of his chief minister Polonius, to go traveling in France, but refuses permission for Hamlet to return to university at Wittenburg. Claudius doesn't want Hamlet out of his sight.

Claudius makes a point of playing father to Hamlet, not only offering paternal advice about getting over his grief, but also repeatedly calling him son. It is as if he wants to redefine their relationship and erase old Hamlet from the picture. But, Hamlet, of course, strongly resists the offered role of becoming Claudius's son. When Claudius tries to offer himself as a father to Hamlet, he responds, "a little more than kin and less than kind." Claudius is too close kin for comfort now he's married Hamlet's mother, and is not only someone whose action is unkind in the sense that it is hurtful to Hamlet, but also unkind in the early 17th-century sense of unnatural.

At the same time as Claudius is acting in this proprietary fashion, Hamlet's mother gently suggests that he's overplaying the part of the mourning son to his dead father. If everyone must go through the experience of losing a parent, why is he insisting on the uniqueness of his grief? "Why seems it so particular with thee?" says Gertrude. Hamlet seizes upon the word *seems*. "Seems madam? Nay, it is, I know not seems."

His black clothes, his tears and sad expressions constitute seeming. "An actor might play a part thus," he says, "but, I have that within which passeth show. These but the trappings and the suits of woe." I'm not just acting grief-stricken, my black clothes aren't just a costume; this isn't a mere performance. If you unfold me, you'll find inside and outside match. Except, of course, he doesn't tell her everything that is making him so wretched, the stuff that goes beyond any possible display, that "passeth show." We learn about that in his first soliloquy. Let's listen to Hamlet once he is on his own:

> "O, that this too too solid flesh would melt, thaw and resolve itself into a dew. Or that the everlasting had not fixed his canon against self-slaughter. O God. God. How weary, stale, flat and unprofitable seem to me all the uses of this world. Fie on it. Fie. 'Tis an unweeded garden, that grows to seed; things rank and gross in nature possess it merely. That it

should come to this. But two months dead. Nay, not so much, not two. So excellent a king; that was, to this, Hyperion to a satyr. So loving to my mother that he might not beteem the winds of heaven visit her face too roughly. Heaven and earth! Must I remember? Why, she would hang on him, as if increase of appetite had grown by what it fed on and yet, within a month—Let me not think on it. Frailty, thy name is woman. A little month, or ere those shoes were old with which she followed my poor father's body, like Niobe, all tears. Why she, even she. O, God. A beast, that wants discourse of reason, would have mourned longer, married with my uncle, my father's brother... O, most wicked speed, to post with such dexterity to incestuous sheets. It is not, nor it cannot come to good, but break my heart, for I must hold my tongue."

The soliloquy, the speech alone, the speech of self-reflection, is by dramatic convention a space of truth telling, of soul-baring. Even the villains speak the truth in soliloquy. Let's ponder the mood established by Hamlet's first soliloquy. He wants to die. He wishes that he wouldn't be risking damnation by committing suicide. Our hero is utterly disgusted with his continued existence: "How weary, flat, stale, and unprofitable, Seem to me all the uses of this world." In a thoroughly alienated manner, he describes the world as an "unweeded garden," gone to seed, rank, wild, disorderly. And as we get the story of Gertrude and Claudius's marriage retold in Hamlet's terms, it becomes clear that they are the things rank and gross in nature who seem to be infecting Hamlet's universe. He obsesses over Gertrude's speedy remarriage, harping on the shortness of time between his father's funeral and her wedding to Claudius, the time he seems to telescope and gets shorter as he speaks of it. He presents Claudius as the absolute opposite to his father. His father was like Hyperion—that is Apollo, the sun God. Claudius is, he says, a satyr, a lustful creature, half animal, half man. Is this the objective truth of the matter, or is Hamlet's grief insisting on the extremity of Claudius's otherness?

His mother, by implication, is less than a beast. A beast, he says, would have mourned longer than she did. It's a very uncomfortable speech for the hearer. Hamlet seems horrified by the very fact of his mother's sexuality and by her refusal to discriminate between his father and Claudius as objects of her desire. Note how he generalizes about all women from her actions. "Frailty"—by this he means sort of sexual promiscuity almost or just general moral frailty—"frailty, thy name is woman," which reminds us how young he is, this kind of splendid generalization, this rather irrational leap of logic. You'll note, however, that whatever distresses him, the fact that he hasn't become king is not at the forefront of his mind. He doesn't talk at all about Claudius being king rather than himself.

And with one of the telling juxtapositions at which Shakespeare excels, the very next scene offers us another young man also worrying about female sexuality. Laertes, rather pompously and urbanely advises his sister Ophelia to distrust Hamlet's kindnesses to her, which brings us to another of the play's secrets. What exactly has passed between Hamlet and Ophelia before the action opens? It's something a director is going to have to decide before he shapes his own performance of the play, and in Kenneth Branagh's movie, for example, Branagh offered silent flashbacks in which Hamlet and Ophelia were being very intimate and loving, which that relationship was clearly sexual.

At any rate, Laertes and Polonius assume that Hamlet's intentions towards Ophelia must be dishonorable. Do not believe his vows, says Polonius. He's a prince. He will have to make a political marriage. He's only trying to beguile you, to seduce you. But, why should he be so assured of his opinion? Have we seen anything in Hamlet that suggests he's a callous and dishonorable womanizer? They seem to consider Hamlet only in terms of his political position, not as an individual who might love honorably. Polonius gives all sorts of fatherly advice to Laertes, concluding, famously, "to thine own self be true." But, he will not let Ophelia be true to herself, to act upon her belief that Hamlet's intentions are honorable.

There are some ironies here. We will later see Polonius himself sending off a kind of surveillance guy to check out what Laertes is up to in France, and that Polonius isn't a wise benign old man is suggested, perhaps, by his behavior with Ophelia, adding his own warnings to those of Laertes. He never says be careful because I don't want you to get hurt; his emphasis is on the fact that he doesn't want his property harmed. In Shakespeare's time, a woman of noble birth would be worthless on the marriage market without her virginity.

But even as he notes that Hamlet can, in any case, have more freedom of action than a young woman, because of his rank, because of his sex, Polonius's language is suggestive: "He is young, and with a larger tether may he walk than may be given to you." Within a larger tether he may walk. He has more freedom than her, but he's still on a leash. The older generation seeks to control the young in this play. While most of the men, whatever their age, want to control the sexuality of their kinswomen. All the early scenes of parents advising and seeking to control children climax in Hamlet's encounter with the ghost. You can't escape your parents, even when they're dead, in this play.

But, I want to skip for a moment to the very end of the encounter with the ghost. You may remember that when Hamlet gets Horatio and Marcellus to swear to reveal nothing of what they have seen that night, the ghost's voice is heard beneath their feet repeating the prince's command, "Swear!" And in response to this voice from the underworld, these notes from underground, Hamlet says, "Well said, old mole." Old mole. In this episode, Hamlet refers to the ghost as both a mole and also as a pioneer—that is, as a burrowing animal, and using the 17th-century term for a mining engineer. A pioneer was at that time a military digger of trenches. So, is this a being that undermines, subverts from below, a voice from hell? What's status of the ghost anyway?

The ghost tells Hamlet that he only walks at night. In the daytime, he is confined to suffer in fires until the sins he has committed during his lifetime have been burnt and purged away. He is invoking here the doctrine of purgatory. In Catholic belief of this time, the notion that a period of suffering and purging of sins must be endured before a soul might attain heaven. But, in Shakespeare's England, reformation England, Protestantism had declared the notion of purgatory to be no longer valid. How are we to take this reference to it? Is it supposed to make the audience of the play in 17th-century Protestant England suspicious of the ghost's claims? It has, after all, encouraged Hamlet to do murder. Is it Hamlet whom it is tempting to sin? Is it Hamlet it is undermining? For the ghost unfolds knowledge, which destroys innocence.

I want to think more about the ghost's terrible gift of knowledge. When, in Act 2, we see that Hamlet has not, after all, been able to carry out the ghost's behests immediately. Is this because there was something lacking in Hamlet from the start, or is it the story and the command that the ghost unfolds that corrupts or undermines or paralyzes Hamlet?

We might consider in relation to this a remark Marcellus makes just before Hamlet leaves to speak to the ghost alone. "Something is rotten in the state of Denmark," he says. Ghosts don't walk when all is well with the world. His words seem to echo Hamlet's image of his universe as a rank, poisonously overgrown garden. Marcellus is referring to his country, but note that it's possible that Denmark can mean the king of Denmark. Something may also be rotten in the state—that is, condition—of the king of Denmark. Marcellus speaks truer than he realizes. For Hamlet learns that not only is the current Denmark, Uncle Claudius, hiding evil behind his genial appearance, but that Claudius literally made something rotten in the state of Denmark. That is, he corrupted the physical condition of Hamlet's father, killing him with a poison, which made a horrible skin disease cover his entire body.

Shakespeare takes this image of a corruption of both ruler and state even further. The ghost tells Hamlet that the official bulletin about his death declares that he was stung by a serpent while sleeping in his orchard and says, "So, the whole ear of Denmark is by a forged process of my death, rankly abused." To abuse, in this context, means to misuse, to corrupt. Claudius poured his poison into the king of Denmark's ear, but the ear of the whole country, the political body of Denmark, has also been poisoned by the false story of his death.

Sixteenth and 17th-century authors regularly imagine the state as an organism comparable to a human body, or speak of the monarch's body as being continuous with the state. This is the notion of the body politic. Watch out for other images in this play of corruption and disease that seethe beneath the surface of both the state and its people, and consider the following. The ghost says that he will not unfold the terrors of purgatory, the secrets of his prison house, because it is forbidden him and it would be too much for Hamlet to bear. But it, nevertheless, leaves Hamlet in a kind of hell, which is exactly what Horatio feared when he told him not to follow the ghost, lest it draw him into madness. The ghost unfolds to Hamlet what he, in fact, already half knows. The official version of his father's death was that he was stung by a serpent while sleeping in the palace gardens, "But know, thou noble youth, the serpent that did sting thy father's life, now wears his crown." "Oh my prophetic soul," responds Hamlet, "mine uncle!" Is the ghost the prophetic soul, or has Hamlet's own soul been prophesying?

And then the ghost gives him his orders. Don't let this state of things continue, he says. "Let not the royal bed of Denmark be a couch for luxury and damned incest. But, howsoever thou pursuest this act, taint not thy mind, nor let thy soul contrive against thy mother aught." It's an impossible commission, taint not thy mind and at the same time don't contrive any action against your mother. Don't let your revenge touch her. Don't let your soul dwell on her sins. Hamlet's own ear has been poisoned by the ghost's history. Can his mind possibly not be tainted? How can he possibly separate the revenge on Claudius from his problematic relations with Gertrude? Especially since his first soliloquy showed us how obsessed he was with his mother's remarriage. When he speaks of what he has learned about Gertrude and Claudius after the ghost's disappearance, note it's Gertrude whom he upbraids first, "O most pernicious woman," only then turning to his uncle, "O villain, villain, smiling, damned villain."

The ghost said, "Remember me." Let's see what Hamlet has to say about this:

> "Remember thee? Yea, from the table of my memory I'll wipe away all trivial fond records, all saws of books, all forms, all pressures past that youth and observation copied there, and thy commandment all alone shall live within the book and volume of my brain."

The table of his memory, the image is of a writing tablet where one might copy down useful bits of information, wise sayings, observations on things that were important to one. Remembering, the act of memorializing the ghost, seems to require from Hamlet the wiping out of all other memories, of his very sense of his own identity. He has to forget himself. He swears to become a new person, a revenger. He must erase all ties, bonds, relations. They get reduced to, dismissed as trivial fond records. Does Hamlet suggest that the ghost is asking him to become something less than human? Certainly, he is no longer his own man, for, as an instrument of vengeance, he is going to have to become, in some sense, the living equivalent of his father who manifests in armor, as a warrior. But, we have already heard Hamlet say that he isn't a warrior. In his first soliloquy, he declares that Claudius is no more like his father than he, Hamlet, is like the great mythical hero Hercules, and all he wanted to do was to go back to his university life.

Hamlet's own language suggests how utterly uncongenial, how absolutely self-alienating the ghost's commands must be to him. At the very end of the scene, he declares, "The time is out of joint. O cursed spite that ever I was born to set it right." He is commanded to act, but according to somebody else's script, playing an unchosen part that he frets against. Why has he ended up being fingered by destiny as the avenging son? We have already learned that he loathes the idea of merely seeming. He's furious when his mother suggests he's putting on a rather too elaborate performance of his grief for his dead father. But, he is now going to have to dissimulate and hide the horrible knowledge he has been given. Now, he indeed has "that within which passeth show."

"The time is out of joint. O cursed spite that ever I was born to set it right." Whose is the spite in the end? Claudius's? His father's? Some cruel and unfeeling cosmic power that has put him in this position? Claudius had tried to take on old Hamlet's identity as Hamlet's father and who commanded the prince to stay in Denmark, to act against his own desires and temperament—to be a courtier, not a scholar. Is the ghost of his father doing exactly the same thing in demanding that he turn himself into a version of the dead warrior, refusing him a self, an identity of his own? Claudius poured poison into King Hamlet's ear. Are we getting a horrible replay of that event now that the ghost has poured poison into his own son's ear? How does Shakespeare himself want us to feel about the morality of revenge? Well, that's something I shall turn to in my next lecture.

Lecture Four
Hamlet II—The Performance of Revenge

Scope:

This lecture discusses the multiple perspectives *Hamlet* offers on the figure of the revenger and analyzes the play's complex exploration of the morality of revenge. Looking at the multiplying and competing acts of "plotting" within the work—and at the arrival of the players and Hamlet's exploitation of their performance for his own ends—it explores Shakespeare's interest in relationships among acting, revenge, and moral agency. Why is Hamlet so good at "acting" (that is, dissembling, role-playing) and so bad at turning the desire for revenge into the performance of revenge? Is his unwillingness to kill Claudius precipitately a sin or a virtue?

Outline

I. Laertes's eagerness to avenge Polonius's death allows Shakespeare to explore and critique the notion that revenge is a "heroic" action.

    A. Laertes, unlike Hamlet, seems untroubled by qualms of conscience and acts without hesitation, but his obsession with revenge allows Claudius to make him his tool.

    B. When Hamlet acts most like Laertes—impulsively, violently—he kills the wrong man and sets in motion the events that will lead to his death.

    C. To be bent on killing is always morally problematic: the revenger defies the dictates of Scripture when he takes over the role of divine justice, seeking to play God.

    D. Ironically, when Hamlet tells Gertrude that the heavens have made him their "scourge and minister," he does so after mistakenly killing Polonius.

II. Shakespeare is interested in exploring (and interrogating) the free agency of the revenger.

    A. Laertes thinks he's fulfilling his own will and desires but is, in fact, serving Claudius's purposes.

    B. Hamlet praises the man who is not "passion's slave" and who is unswayed by external forces, but his own situation is impossibly complicated.

1. He is caught up in a set of events he didn't initiate and is commanded to do murder by a force beyond the grave.

2. He is increasingly the object of plots initiated by Claudius, and he is surrounded by spies.

3. Hamlet's will to action is also affected by his own intellect and emotions.

C. The complexity of Hamlet's situation suggests that the most powerful tragic dramas are those in which the protagonist is under the greatest pressure from a combination of *external and internal* forces.

D. It is not surprising that Hamlet contemplates suicide because his death may be the only thing he feels he has any control over.

III. Hamlet's speeches of self-interrogation—and the soliloquies in which he lacerates himself for failing to exact bloody vengeance—often set (ostensibly) noble *action* in a complicated relationship with mere *acting*: dissembling and role-playing.

A. Shakespeare is here putting his own spin on a popular contemporary metaphor describing existence as a stage play (a metaphor often invoked in his other dramas).

B. An impromptu performance by the professional players leads Hamlet to contrast an actor's weeping for Queen Hecuba's fictional sufferings to his own inability to respond to a very real "cue for passion."

C. Hamlet does not, however, turn away from theatricality: he deploys it to find out the truth of Claudius's actions.

1. He hopes his rewrite of *The Murder of Gonzago*, in mirroring his uncle's murderous actions, will move Claudius to betray his guilt—although this "mirroring" is complicated when Hamlet makes the murderer the nephew of the poisoned king.

2. Hamlet feels the need to be assured of Claudius's guilt, lest the Ghost be an emissary of the devil tempting him to damn himself through murder.

D. Hamlet's request that the chief player deliver a speech about

Pyrrhus is interesting: the brutally vengeful Pyrrhus offers yet another problematic foil for Hamlet-as-revenger.

IV. Hamlet is himself an actor when he deploys his "antic disposition," his feigned madness.

    A. His crazed behavior will help him to mask his dangerous knowledge of his father's murder.

    B. However, conversing with Rosencrantz and Guildenstern, Hamlet seems to articulate a melancholic vision remarkably similar to the one he voiced in his first soliloquy.

    C. The slippery borderline between performance and reality is also suggested by his aggressive behavior to Ophelia in the nunnery scene.

V. Hamlet as would-be man of action is juxtaposed not only with Laertes but also with Fortinbras.

    A. Sent on a mission to England by Claudius, Hamlet encounters the army of Fortinbras.

    B. When Hamlet learns that Fortinbras and his men are risking their lives to recapture a meager bit of territory, he is moved to compare his own hesitations with their valiance.

    C. At the same time that he seems to find Fortinbras' actions heroic, Hamlet betrays in his soliloquy some skepticism concerning the rash courage that risks others' lives "even for an eggshell."

    D. Shakespeare offers us the possibility that Hamlet's scruples may be more admirable than the unthinking violence of Fortinbras and Laertes.

    E. Hamlet's world celebrates the warrior ethos that justifies destructive action when personal honor seems to be at stake. The question remains whether Hamlet can in fact play out the "Fortinbras script."

Essential Reading:

Shakespeare, *Hamlet*.

Supplementary Reading:

Kerrigan, *Revenge Tragedy: Aeschylus to Armageddon*, pp. 181–192.

Mangan, *A Preface to Shakespeare's Tragedies*, pp. 133–141.

Questions to Consider:

1. What advice on acting does Hamlet give the players before they stage the "play within the play"? Can you relate his concerns here to his other meditations on what it means to *act* (in both senses of the word)?

2. How does Hamlet exploit his assumed "antic disposition" to particular effect in his conversations with the various characters who are spying on his doings?

Lecture Four—Transcript
Hamlet II—The Performance of Revenge

In Act 4, scene 5 of *Hamlet*, Laertes, having heard of his father's death and desperate to find out who is responsible for it, comes charging back from France, stirs up a mob of supporters, and invades the palace. He does not pause for a soliloquy. "How came he dead? I'll not be juggled with. To hell, allegiance! Vows to the blackest devil! Conscience and grace to the profoundest pit! I dare damnation... Let come what comes. Only I'll be revenged most thoroughly for my father." Laertes doesn't care about the moral consequences of taking his revenge. He dispatches his conscience to hell and says I dare damnation. This is very different from Hamlet's scrupulous worrying about whether the ghost he's seen is really his father's spirit or an emissary from the devil seeking to tempt him to murder.

Laertes appears to be better qualified to be the hero of an orthodox revenge tragedy than Hamlet. But, the play isn't called *The Tragedy of Laertes, Nobleman of Denmark*. Shakespeare has chosen to explore what happens when an intelligent, sensitive, thoughtful man, who knows that actions have consequences and is concerned about the moral status of those actions, is asked to play a role that is entirely alien to his own nature. Indeed, it is on the one occasion that Hamlet acts most like Laertes—impulsively, violently—that he ends up causing the most havoc. That is, when he lunges out at the tapestry in his mother's bedroom, thinking Claudius is concealed behind it and finds it is Laertes's father that he has killed. And this is a watershed moment in the play. By killing Polonius, Hamlet himself becomes a man of blood, implicated in the pattern of wanton killings in Denmark. His action drives Ophelia into madness and sets in motion the train of events, which will lead to his own death at Laertes's hands.

Shakespeare offers us the much more conventional revenger, Laertes, as a foil to the prince, using him to critique the notion that revenge is necessarily a heroic action, because think what happens to the reckless Laertes. His passion for revenge allows Claudius to manipulate him easily. Before he knows it, he has become the king's tool. He starts by insisting that his honor requires that he carry out this revenge, that if he remains calm in the face of his father's death, he isn't his father's son. But, Claudius's proposition to Laertes is hardly honorable. He persuades him to arrange what will look like a kind of exhibition fencing match between himself and Hamlet, but one at which Laertes's sword will accidentally be unbated—that is, it won't be the blunt sword used for practice fights. Upon which Laertes proposes that his sword will not just be unbated, but poisoned. "I'll touch my point with this contagion, that if I gall him slightly it may be death." Poison and contagion and disease again. Laertes, in enthusiastically agreeing to Claudius's plan and then giving it a spin of his own, has become a part of the rot in Denmark.

The ghost said to Hamlet, don't taint your mind as you follow my commands, an impossible proposition. To be bent on murder is to be contaminated, in some sense. The universe of the play is indeed an officially Christian universe and revenge is officially forbidden in a Christian universe. We have the biblical injunction, "Thou shalt not kill," and the verse of the Bible most usually quoted in respect to revenge is from chapter 12 of St. Paul's Epistle to the Romans, verse 19: "Dearly beloved, avenge not yourselves…for it is written, Vengeance is mine; I will repay, saith the Lord," which are perhaps some of the most ignored words in the New Testament.

A revenger takes over the role of divine justice; he seeks to play God. Hamlet, indeed, will tell Gertrude that he is the heavens' scourge and minister, their agent who is carrying out God's punishments on earth. Ironically, he says this to her after he has killed the wrong person. Laertes thinks he's a heroic revenger fulfilling his own will and desires, but Claudius quickly starts scripting his actions, and his mind becomes as poisoned as the sword he'll use on Hamlet. Let's pursue this matter of revengers acting within other people's scripts a little further. In his tragedies, Shakespeare is particularly interested in exploring the whole issue of human agency. What shapes and what inhibits our actions? To what extent are our actions the products of our own free will and choice? To what extent are they determined by other people's actions or by social, political, cultural and even cosmic forces external to us?

Hamlet, praising his friend Horatio's character, honors the man who is not passion's slave, who stands alone, unswayed by the winds of fortune—a noble stoic. Laertes is certainly slave to his own passions. He also becomes subject to Claudius's will and desires. Hamlet's own situation is impossibly complicated. He is caught up in a set of events he didn't initiate within a world from which he feels wholly alienated. A force beyond the grave has commanded him on his honor as a loyal son to do certain terrible things. He is increasingly the object of plots initiated by Claudius. He is surrounded by people spying on his actions, and his will to action is also going to be affected by his own nature. There are forces within him that are going to shape what he does. I'd suggest to you, in fact, that the most powerful tragic dramas are those in which the protagonist is under the greatest pressure from a combination of external and internal forces.

It is not surprising, perhaps, that Hamlet has two soliloquies in which he contemplates suicide. His death may be the only thing he feels he has any control over. Famously, in the "to be or not to be" soliloquy, he is brought up short when he meditates upon the scary unknown of what comes next, the undiscovered country of the afterlife, the territory from which no traveler returns. He's trapped in a nightmarish existence, but worse might await. He tries to persuade himself that to die is simply to enter a final sleep, but in the sleep of death, what dreams might come?

The multiplicity of forces and circumstances impinging upon Hamlet's doings are suggested by the many and competing plots and performances devised by the play's characters. We have multiple plotters. Claudius orchestrates the treacherous duel. The ghost plots revenge and plots the cleansing of the monarchy. Hamlet plots to use a theatrical performance to nudge Claudius into revealing his guilt, and also puts everybody on edge with his extended performance of the antic disposition, that is, his faked madness. The king and queen give Rosencrantz and Guildenstern a script to follow as they command them to try to get Hamlet to reveal the cause of his melancholy. The king and Polonius stage two encounters to find out more about Hamlet's state of mind. First, the loosing of Ophelia to him, while Claudius and Polonius spy on their encounter. Later, the interrogation of Hamlet by Gertrude while Polonius listens behind the tapestry. Hamlet rewrites this particular script, of course, when, thinking it is Claudius lurking behind the curtain, he kills Polonius.

The play keeps showing us its hero's interrogation of his actions, his renewed attempts to fulfill the ghost's commands, his self-laceration for his failure to act. At the same time, it interweaves the notion of heroic action with that of another kind of acting, dissembling, feigning, counterfeiting. It's not perhaps surprising this comes up so much; the very notion of comparing existence to a stage play is a particular favorite in Renaissance England, and you might think of references to this in Shakespeare's other plays. "All the world's a stage and all the men and women are merely players," says Jaques in *As You Like It*. Macbeth, of course, compares life to a poor player that struts and frets his hour upon the stage.

When the professional players arrive at Elsinore, Hamlet asks their leader to deliver a speech from a play in which a character is describing the last terrible night of the Trojan War. He is speaking of the Greeks' sacking of the city and the climactic moment when Pyrrhus, the son of the Greek hero Achilles, kills King Priam of Troy in revenge for his own father's death. The speech ends with a description of Queen Hecuba lamenting the butchering of her husband. Polonius, who is not the world's most sophisticated drama critic, exclaims at the fact that the actor is weeping as he speaks.

In the soliloquy Hamlet speaks after everybody has left, he is very much struck by the implications of this. "Is it not monstrous that this player here, but in a fiction, in a dream of passion could force his soul so to his own conceit? Tears in his eyes, distraction in his aspect. A broken voice. What's Hecuba to him, or he to Hecuba, that he should weep for her? What would he do had he the motive and the cue for passion that I have?" How can he, Hamlet, do nothing when the player, but in a fiction, in a dream of passion, has displayed such grief? What's Hecuba to him, or he to Hecuba? What does it mean that he, Hamlet, is silent about the death of his father, and has done nothing to avenge it?

But, Hamlet doesn't then rush off to kill Claudius. Having drawn our attention to the gap between the players' fabricated emotion and his own very real motive and cue for passion, he doesn't turn away from counterfeiting, from acting, from pretending he doesn't know what he knows. He instead tries to exploit the possibilities of counterfeiting, of acting, of theatricality. He will have the players reenact the murder of his father and observe Claudius's reaction. "I have heard that guilty creatures sitting at a play have by the very cunning of the scene been struck so to the soul that presently they have proclaimed their malefactions." His art will hold a mirror up to nature and Hamlet will invite Claudius to see himself in the drama he stages for the court, to acknowledge his own crimes. "If he but blench, I know my course." If Claudius just turns pale, he'll know what to do, and we might recall here Sidney's definition of tragedy: "The high and excellent tragedy, that openeth the greatest wounds, and showeth forth the ulcers that are covered with tissue. That maketh kings fear to be tyrants and tyrants manifest their tyrannical humors."

But, the mirror presented by Hamlet's rewrite of *The Murder of Gonzago* is an interestingly skewed one. We do have a murdered king and a faithless queen, but who is the third character? As the little play is performed to the court, Hamlet offers a running commentary, and as the player who will murder the king enters, he says, "This is one Lucianus, nephew to the king"—that is, the murderer of the king in Hamlet's play is not the king's brother, but the king's nephew.

The play within a play could be thought of as showing Claudius killing his brother and then seducing his sister-in-law, or, alternatively, it could be showing Hamlet, the nephew of Claudius, killing Claudius and reclaiming his mother from him. Did Hamlet consciously mean to alter the original scenario? And what exactly has terrified Claudius when he calls for lights, lights, and flees the room?

Let's go back to the soliloquy at the end of Act 2, and look a little more at Hamlet's lingering doubts about the ghost in that speech. After deciding to stage a play that reenacts his father's death, he says:

> "The spirit that I have seen may be the devil, and the devil hath power to assume a pleasing shape. Yea, and perhaps out of my weakness and my melancholy...abuses me to damn me. I'll have grounds more relative than this. The play's the thing wherein I'll catch the conscience of the king."

Hamlet has been asked to play the role of revenger, but it has to be his own action done on his own terms. He starts this long soliloquy cursing himself for his inertia, but he ends it insisting he doesn't want to be the tool of any dark force.

Something else we might note: On the one hand, the player offers Hamlet a stimulus to action. If he can be so moved by the tears of a fictional queen, why can't I be moved to action by the real death of my father? But, the players' bombastic set piece also offers a very repellent vision of a revenger in action. The frenzied Pyrrhus who chops up the limbs of old Priam with his sword. Pyrrhus constitutes another problematic alter ego for Hamlet, a fourth revenger to set beside Fortinbras and Laertes. Shakespeare's deployment of all these reflections and refractions of Hamlet's situation keeps obliging us to interrogate the morality of revenge. Hamlet ends his soliloquy by deciding to use feigning and indirect methods to justify his own vengeance. In pretending only to be putting on an entertainment for the court, he'll continue to act, to dissemble, rather than to take violent and direct action.

So, let's think a bit more about Hamlet, the actor. The most striking example of Hamlet's acting is his supposed madness. After he's seen the ghost, Hamlet warns Horatio and Marcellus that, in future, he may choose to feign insanity and to put on what he calls an antic disposition. There's an obvious logic behind this. He knows too much and he has to conceal what he knows. He can't possibly just act naturally, so he will act as if he's thoroughly crazy. But, if one looks closely at just how he enacts his supposed condition, some interesting things come into focus. For example, when Rosencrantz and Guildenstern—those Renaissance frat boys—show up at court and Hamlet realizes that they have been set upon him to uncover the cause of his troubled mind, he offers a kind of self-diagnosis for their benefit. "I have of late, but wherefore I know not, lost all my mirth." He goes on to say that all that is beautiful in the universe now looks hideous to him. "What a piece of work is a man? How noble in reason, how infinite in faculty, in action how like an angel, in apprehension how like a god, the beauty of the world, the paragon of animals. And yet to me, what is this quintessence of dust? Man delights not me, nor woman neither."

I'm going through a serious existential crisis; I haven't a clue why, but it has put me in a condition of chronic melancholy, alienated from all humanity. In context, it might be offered as a safely generalized answer to stop Rosencrantz and Guildenstern's proddings and to get them off his back, with a little joke in the end to show them he's still their witty friend. But, if you think about it, he's reporting exactly the condition he described in Act 1, before he started to feign madness. Remember the words he spoke from the heart in his first soliloquy: "How weary, flat, stale and unprofitable seem to me all the uses of this world." Is the vision he offered in that first soliloquy really so different from the condition of anomie he describes to Rosencrantz and Guildenstern?

That is, the act he's putting on for the benefit of all the court spies is pretty close to his own previous reality. So, what is performance, what is reality? Hamlet's actions are at their most ambiguous perhaps in the nasty scene in which the wretched Ophelia is shoved into his path and he abuses her, makes her part of a general indictment of the deceits of women, and ends by telling her to get herself off to a nunnery. In Shakespearian English, a nunnery is the slang term for a brothel. He really seems to have lost it. It's hard to draw the line between performance and pathology at this moment. But, whom is he actually talking to in this scene?

The whole encounter with Ophelia was carefully planned between Claudius and Polonius in Act 2, scene 2, and in that scene Hamlet enters at the end of their conversation. Does he hear anything of their plans? And this is another problem that a director will have to resolve for him or herself. The Olivier film version of *Hamlet*, in that the camera shows Hamlet quite clearly overhearing the exchange between the king and Polonius.

When Hamlet castigates Ophelia in Act 3, scene 1, some of his lines do seem strongly to hint at an awareness he's being spied on. He suddenly says out of nowhere to her, where's your father? And, of course, Ophelia is all too aware that her father is lurking and listening. And then, he goes off on that rant in which he says, "I say we will have no more marriages. Those that are married already, all but one, shall live. The rest shall keep as they are." Those that are married already, all but one, shall live. Claudius might not like the sound of that. Hamlet might be seen here as a very skillful actor, speaking to one audience while also directing some jibes at another, without ever quite betraying that he knows himself to be under surveillance. But, he himself is repeatedly fearful that he is only acting, in the most problematic sense of just posturing, just playing a role.

I started this lecture by comparing Laertes and Hamlet. I'd now like to return to a doubling I pointed out between Hamlet and Fortinbras, another angry young man. They almost, but don't quite meet in Act

4, scene 4. Their not quite meeting triggers more of Hamlet's meditations on the problem of acting and action.

Fortinbras has been packed off by his uncle on a military mission to Poland. Hamlet, who has been packed off by his uncle on a diplomatic mission to England watches Fortinbras's troops marching towards Poland and asks what's going on. He's told that they're going to try to win back a small and worthless patch of disputed territory, which the Poles are defending fiercely. Hamlet, as he did with the player's speech about Hecuba, makes this information the starting point for some reflections of his own. Soliloquizing about what he has seen, he wrestles with his own apparent inability to play the revenger:

> "Now, whether it be bestial oblivion or some craven scruple of thinking too precisely on the event… I do not know why yet I live to say, 'This thing's to do,' sith I have cause, and will, and strength, and means to do't. Examples gross as earth exhort me. Witness this army of such mass and charge, led by a delicate and tender prince, whose spirit, with divine ambition puffed, makes mouths at the invisible event, exposing what is mortal and unsure to all that fortune, death, and danger dare, even for an eggshell… How stand I then, that have a father killed, a mother stained, excitements of my reason and my blood, and let all sleep? While to my shame I see the imminent death of twenty thousand men that for a fantasy and trick of fame go to their graves like beds."

This is a very double-edged speech. Whether it is a kind of cowardice, says Hamlet, or whether it is that I am being too conscience-stricken and scrupulous, or whether it is that I am worrying too much about what I'll face after killing my uncle, whatever it is, I'm still talking, not acting. Here is a brave, ambitious young prince who risks everything even for an eggshell. I have an urgent reason to use violence, but do nothing, and now I see Fortinbras's whole army facing death for a fantasy and a trick of fame, fighting over a bit of land not big enough to bury them all because they think it is the honorable thing to do.

But, as Hamlet exhorts himself to take action, to play the role of revenger properly, his argument is oddly self-subverting. He berates himself for fretting about the consequences of his actions, for thinking too precisely on the event and not making a move. But, is this his problem? Does this speak to some lack in him, or are his scruples what make him more fully human than a Laertes or a Fortinbras?

Hamlet's world values the warrior ethos, which justifies destructive action when personal honor seems to be at stake. Hamlet, at times, seems to try to toe the party line, but his intellect and imagination persist in implicitly or explicitly interrogating the very ethos he is trying to imitate. Here he seems to wish to emulate the heroic warrior, tearing off to fight over an eggshell. But, his own thought processes, his own words, his metaphors, betray him. They set up a countercurrent to his purported desires. Look at the images he evokes. Fighting over an eggshell. Going to one's death for a fantasy or a trick of fame. His language keeps evoking a very futile kind of violence. Can Fortinbras really be a role model? Hamlet ends his soliloquy with another assertion of renewed aggression: "O, from this time forth, my thoughts be bloody, or be nothing worth." It's pretty melodramatic stuff. Can Hamlet really play the Fortinbras script?

Well, I shall eventually be looking at what happens to Hamlet's bloody thoughts of revenge, but in my next lecture, I am going to change my focus a little and explore some of the play's other preoccupations and other characters and, in particular, its much abused women, Gertrude and Ophelia.

Lecture Five
Hamlet III—Difficult Women

Scope:

This lecture takes as its starting point the observation that although Hamlet may be slow to enact his revenge upon Claudius, he is capable of extraordinary emotional violence against his mother and against the young woman he claims to have loved. (It is to them that he "speaks daggers.") The lecture explores Hamlet's confrontations with Gertrude and Ophelia, addressing in particular his preoccupation with their sexuality; it also considers, in passing, the paradox that despite the fact that the "transgressive" actions of women seem to trigger a good deal of crucial action in this play, it is difficult to think of Gertrude and Ophelia as tragic protagonists in their own right. The lecture concludes by comparing Hamlet's dissembled madness, his "antic disposition," with the way that Shakespeare represents Ophelia's actual madness.

Outline

I. *Hamlet* is an enormously capacious play—but it is also a play full of gaps, secrets, and silences, and some of its most baffling aspects concern its female characters.

   A. Although we learn a lot about Hamlet's inner life and hear Claudius revealing his guilty fears in soliloquy, Ophelia and Gertrude have little or no opportunity for self-reflection.

   B. We do not know how Ophelia feels about being told to cease communication with Hamlet, then being used as a tool in Polonius's and Claudius's machinations.

   C. We cannot be entirely sure, when Hamlet tells Gertrude that Claudius murdered his father, whether she thinks he is speaking the truth or speaking in his madness.

II. "Unreadable" as they are, Gertrude and Ophelia do operate as flash points for Hamlet's anger. In Acts 1–3, much of his emotional violence is projected onto and directed at the two women.

   A. In the "nunnery scene," Hamlet verbally savages Ophelia and associates her with all the faults stereotypically ascribed to women in a misogynist culture.

B. Hamlet has been reviling his mother's remarriage since Act 1, and when he is summoned to her chamber, he sidesteps an opportunity to kill Claudius in order to "speak daggers" to Gertrude.

C. As well as disclosing Claudius's guilt, Hamlet dwells unpleasantly upon his vision of Gertrude's sexual relationship with his uncle.

D. In a revenge play ostensibly focused upon the imperative to kill Claudius, Hamlet often behaves as if his mother is the primary transgressor.

E. Even though Shakespeare's culture "policed" women's sexuality very strictly, the degree of Hamlet's disgust at his mother's mature desires cannot be explained by historical difference alone.

III. Interestingly, Shakespeare's own representation of Gertrude is far more sympathetic than Hamlet's characterization of his mother.

A. In 1.2., Gertrude gently tries to persuade Hamlet not to lose himself in grief.

B. In 2.2., she is worried by his ever-more disturbing behavior and shows herself to be well aware of some of the factors that have caused it.

C. Gertrude alone shows kindness to Ophelia when she is being used to bait a trap for Hamlet.

IV. The "closet scene" is a particularly charged moment in the interaction between Hamlet and Gertrude.

A. The fact that Polonius is lurking in a private space that would normally be accessible only by her husband or son confirms that Gertrude is complicit in Claudius's spying on Hamlet.

B. In this scene, Hamlet acts with a violence we do not see again until the very end of the play and lays bare his mother's most intimate acts.

C. Despite the violence of Hamlet's assault on her, Gertrude afterwards describes his actions (to Claudius) in a forgiving light and speaks of him more generously than he ever speaks of her.

V. The situations of Ophelia and Hamlet are in some ways parallel, but there are significant differences in Shakespeare's treatment of their responses to their pain.

 A. Ophelia is not represented as instigating action or agonizing over her choices; her speeches show little of her inner state.

 B. Ophelia, like Hamlet, can articulate her anger or grief in the language of madness that takes her outside the bounds of courtly decorum.

 1. But Hamlet uses his antic disposition to attack other people, elucidate their motives, and mirror back to them their problematic behavior. He operates in dialogue with others.

 2. Ophelia speaks in isolation and in heavily coded language, often through fragments of song.

 3. Hamlet's "antic disposition" causes anxiety and fear in others; Ophelia's madness causes pain and distress, but her actions are ultimately reduced to a pathetic yet pretty spectacle.

VI. The play's treatment of Ophelia's death reinforces this muting of her actions.

 A. Gertrude describes her death in a lyrical speech in which Ophelia disappears into the natural setting where she perished.

 B. Ophelia has little or no agency; the passivity she displays as she drowns differs significantly from the consciously chosen "self-slaughter" Hamlet has contemplated.

Essential Reading:

Shakespeare, *Hamlet.*

Supplementary Reading:

Adelman, *Suffocating Mothers: Fantasies of Maternal Origin in Shakespeare's Plays*, chapter 2.

Showalter, "Representing Ophelia: Women, Madness and the Responsibilities of Feminist Criticism," in *Shakespeare's Middle Tragedies: A Collection of Critical Essays*, David Young, ed., pp. 56–69.

Questions to Consider:

1. Take another look at the scenes in which Ophelia appears prior to Polonius's death. Can you glean anything about her own state of mind and opinions from her few speeches?

2. Why do you think Shakespeare has the ghost reappear in the closet scene? How does its brief appearance affect the dynamics of Hamlet's confrontation with Gertrude?

Lecture Five—Transcript
Hamlet III—Difficult Women

Hamlet is almost never performed in its entirety. An uncut performance would take at least four hours. The film versions directed by Olivier and Zefferelli are very much abridged. When Kenneth Branagh chose to film a complete text of the play, he was doing something quite unprecedented. This play is capacious. It incorporates discussions of the theater and of the theory of acting, meditations on suicide, on female sexuality, on warfare, on free will, fortune, and divine providence, on the powers and limits of human reason, on the nature of the afterlife, on human mortality, human passions, on the discrepancies between seeming and being, on the art of the duel, the phenomenology of ghosts, the relations between fathers and sons, sons and mothers, on the duties of kingship, and the silliness of certain contemporary court fashions. It's got everything in it except the kitchen sink. And yet, it is also a play that seems to be full of gaps, secrets, and silences.

Hamlet insists that he has that within, that "passeth show," but we still get an awful lot of Hamlet on show. His part is one of the two or three longest in all of Shakespeare's plays. And we get something of Claudius's inner life, too, when he finally has the soliloquy, as he tries to pray, that makes it quite clear to the audience that he did kill his brother.

But what about the women in this play? For me, they evoke questions that the text doesn't always or completely answer because, in the speeches they are given, we hardly ever see them disclosing their desires or reflecting upon their experiences. How strong are Ophelia's feelings for Hamlet? How intimate had they been with one another before Polonius interfered in Act 1, scene 3? How does she feel about first having to cut off communication with him and later being used as a tool by her father and king Claudius in their own machinations? Why does the madness caused by her father's death make her speak the way she does to Gertrude, Claudius, and Laertes? Was her death an accident or suicide?

And what about Gertrude? When Hamlet, in his mother's bedchamber, accuses Claudius of murdering his father, he doesn't exactly supply a lot of supporting evidence. Does Gertrude think he is speaking the truth or that this is part of his madness? If she does believe it, what does it do to her feelings for Claudius? How does she feel about her own son lecturing her on her sex life? And why isn't old Hamlet's ghost visible to her?

I ask these questions not to suggest that Shakespeare should have written his play quite differently with either Ophelia or Gertrude at its center, but rather to try to highlight certain artistic choices he did make. One thing in particular interests me. On the one hand, we don't get soliloquies from these women. We don't get them laying bare their private thoughts. They are given far less to say than the main male characters. But, on the other hand, Gertrude and Ophelia do operate as flash points for other people's emotional intensity, particularly that of Hamlet. This play will end with a lot of dead bodies on stage, but a good deal of the emotional violence before the final bloodbath is projected on to and directed at the two women.

Let me try to offer an overview of this particular phenomenon. Hamlet's first soliloquy keeps returning to his mother's swift remarriage, his horror at her slipping between, what he calls, incestuous sheets to embrace his uncle. "A beast…would have mourned longer," he says. After the ghost tells his story, Hamlet cries out against his mother, "O most pernicious woman," before he calls Claudius "damned, damned villain." We should remember, incidentally, that the ghost never suggests that Gertrude was an accessory to or even aware of the murder itself.

One of the first ways in which Hamlet stages his assumed madness is to show up in Ophelia's chamber looking both anguished and threatening. "He took me by the wrist and held me hard," she reports. In the only scene in which we see him alone on stage with Ophelia, he lays into her with enormous verbal violence and cries out, "Get thee to a nunnery!"—which, as I've already mentioned, could mean "Get thee to a brothel!" in Elizabethan slang. Berating her, telling her "I know all about you, about your female artifice and deception," he associates her with all the faults stereotypically ascribed to women in a misogynist culture. He also directs a series of cruel and coarse remarks at her before the staging of the play within a play.

"Lady," he says, "shall I lie in your lap?" This is not the kind of behavior one expects at a court function and Ophelia nervously says, "No, my lord." "I mean, my head upon your lap?" Hamlet says. "Did you think that I meant country matters?"—rustic tumbling on the one hand, but with a hint of an obscene buried pun. And of course, when he's summoned to Gertrude's chamber, Hamlet says, "I will speak daggers to her, but use none." On his way there, he actually has the chance to stick a dagger in Claudius, but he backs out, claiming that, as the king is at his prayers, he might end up in heaven, which is not where Hamlet wishes to send him. Instead, he goes to his mother's room and manhandles and bullies Gertrude until she cries out for help, which is what makes Polonius reveal his presence behind the tapestry.

After he has run Polonius through with his sword, thinking that it was Claudius lurking there, Hamlet brutally tells Gertrude what he thinks of her remarriage and accuses her of being possessed by the filthiest kind of lust. He seems especially appalled at the idea that a woman of mature years could still be interested in sex. I personally find this opinion rather problematic. He dwells upon his vision of her sexual relationship with Claudius. She has chosen to live, he says, "in the rank sweat of an enseamed bed, stewed in corruption, honeying and making love over the nasty sty." His language makes her throw his own metaphor of speaking daggers back at him. She cries out, "These words, like daggers, enter in mine ears."

But in a revenge play, where what is officially at issue is the murder of old Hamlet by Claudius and the question of whether Hamlet should obey the Ghost's command and kill Claudius, it's astonishing how much poetic energy is actually taken up by Hamlet's assaults on female sexuality, as if this is what is primarily rotten in the state of Denmark from Hamlet's point of view. As if Gertrude, in particular, is the main and original transgressor who has precipitated all the horror, and Ophelia is a kind of echo of her. The prince's horrified fascinations with his mother's doings, and the violence that he ends up unleashing in the most private space of her chamber, these are all the more striking because his father's ghost had explicitly ordered him not to act against his mother, to leave her to her own conscience.

Female chastity, not only in the sense of premarital virginity, but also in the sense of monogamy within marriage, was a cultural absolute in Renaissance Europe. There were pragmatic reasons behind the societal double standard, which punished female unchastity much more harshly than male philandering. Inheritance was patrilineal, through the male line. In an age without DNA testing, fathers needed to know that their sons were their own. A man's honor was absolutely bound up with the chastity of his wife. But, Gertrude is probably beyond childbearing years and Hamlet isn't married to her; he's her son. This is, to be sure, a culture where adult males often had authority over all the women in their family. But, there seems to be something very particular, excessive about Hamlet's problems with his mother's sexuality, something that can't be explained simply by invoking historical difference.

It's interesting to ask, does the play itself represent Gertrude with the kind of repulsion with which Hamlet depicts his mother and her actions? The prince comes close to describing her as a depraved, lust-obsessed, heartless animal. But, it's interesting to compare Hamlet's version of Gertrude with Shakespeare's version of Gertrude. We don't hear a lot from Gertrude, but what we do hear is far from horrible. In Act 1, scene 2, she gently tries to persuade Hamlet not to lose himself in his grief. In Act 2, scene 2, she is obviously worried at his ever more disturbing behavior and fervently hopes that Rosencrantz and Guildenstern will bring him out of his melancholy. When Claudius and Polonius are speculating on just what is wrong with Hamlet, Gertrude shows herself to be far from insensitive. Claudius tells her that Polonius has a theory about the cause of Hamlet's mental disturbance and she responds, I doubt. In this context, she means, I believe. "I doubt it is no other but the main, his father's death and our o'er hasty marriage." When Polonius and Claudius are callously setting up Ophelia to bait a trap for Hamlet with no thought to her feelings, Gertrude is the only one who speaks kindly to the young woman. "And for your part Ophelia, I do wish that your good beauties be the happy cause of Hamlet's wildness. So, I shall hope your virtues will bring him to his wounded way again to both our honors." She hopes Ophelia's virtuous love can heal her son. She would obviously not oppose a marriage between them.

Hamlet's is only one voice in the play. It's the most articulate and compelling, but there are others. A play is a dialogic structure; multiple voices offer multiple perspectives. Hamlet's own voice is so powerful that we may find ourselves co-opted, almost kidnapped, into sharing his point of view and ignore the words of other characters that complicate or even contradict it. Of course, from Hamlet's perspective, the thing that damns both Ophelia and Gertrude is the fact that they let themselves be used in the plots of

Claudius and Polonius. This is a world where women are pawns in the bigger chess games played by the men. As I mentioned last time, these are games that can be played in two directions, as when Hamlet uses his conversation with Ophelia to direct jibes at the eavesdropping King Claudius.

Gertrude summons Hamlet to a private conference. Rosencrantz says to the prince that Gertrude "desires to speak with you in her closet ere you go to bed." Now, this is important, Gertrude is not in a little clothes closet, but in her own chamber. The word closet is used for various kinds of relatively private rooms at this time. I should mention that in the 17th century, the space in large palatial establishments is organized rather differently from what we expect of houses. Most of the rooms are public rooms. There's very little, absolutely private space. So, going into the space of the closet is quite a big deal. You're going into intimate space. When Hamlet overhears a noise behind the tapestry, the arras, he assumes it must be Claudius. The only men who would normally be permitted in the queen's bedroom would be her husband or her son. The fact that it is Polonius and that Gertrude is not surprised that it is Polonius immediately reveals his mother's involvement in the surveillance plot. Things, in fact, get pretty crowded in Gertrude's closet. Hamlet is getting into the nooks and crannies of Gertrude's private life. He thinks that he's sharing space with Claudius, whom he considers an interloper in his mother's bed, but is, in fact, doing so with a nosy old man who takes far too much interest in people's private doings. Then, later in the scene, the ghost appears to Hamlet for the second time—that is, Gertrude's other husband materializes, as if he's running an intervention to get Hamlet back on track again, to make him reassume the proper role of vengeful son, not to hang around playing something rather close to an angry husband.

Here's one last observation about Gertrude. When Claudius enters in the next scene and finds her weeping, she covers for Hamlet. She says it was his madness that had led him to attack the tapestry and kill Polonius, and when Claudius asks where her son has gone now, she says he's gone to bear off Polonius's body, adding that, even in the midst of his madness, Hamlet is weeping for what he has done. Well, is he? If you glance back at the end of the previous scene, Hamlet's final speech to Gertrude goes as follows: "I'll lug the guts,"—that's not a very nice way to talk about a dead body—"I'll lug the guts into the neighbor room. Mother, good night indeed. This counselor is now most still, most secret, and most grave, who was in life a foolish prating knave,"—which is a pretty brutal epitaph for Polonius, now reduced to a heap of guts by Hamlet's language. There's not much weeping here. Gertrude's language about Hamlet is far more gentle and forgiving than his is ever about her.

Alright, I'd now like to turn to the play's other woman, Ophelia. There are some interesting similarities between Hamlet's situation and Ophelia's. In Act 1, Hamlet and Ophelia are both given commands that they are reluctant to obey by their fathers. They both lose their fathers to violence. Hamlet is swamped in melancholy, assumes the appearance of madness, and contemplates suicide. Ophelia succumbs to actual madness and dies in dubious circumstances that may be, in effect, suicide. But, although there are some teasing parallels between Ophelia and Hamlet's situations, the dramatic presence of Ophelia is of course nothing like that of Hamlet in the play. We don't see her agonizing over her options. She doesn't appear even to have choices to make or, at least, they're not dramatized as such. She's given no speeches, apart from perhaps the brief lament after the nunnery scene that revealed the agony of her own inner state. She has little or no agency. She doesn't set plots in motion; she doesn't instigate action.

Now, of course, young women in early modern Europe are not really supposed to have agency. The holy trinity of virtues held up to them in books prescribing female proper conduct consists of chastity, silence, and obedience. Ophelia says she has done nothing inappropriate with Hamlet, or, at least, that his treatment of her has been honorable, but she obeys her father. She's in a lose-lose situation, to be sure. In properly, according to the conduct books of the time, obeying her father and shunning Hamlet, she becomes an object of disgust to the man she loves. But, the play gives her no space to address her dilemma until she loses her mind. Once insane, she's outside the pale of courtly behavior, of proper female behavior. She can say what she wants. She can take center stage. She has her own antic disposition as a mask.

When Hamlet is performing his antic disposition, he uses language to attack other people, to fence with them, to find out their weaknesses and the true motives behind their actions and to make his own points, and also to mirror what is problematic in their behavior back to them.

His madness, whether it be assumed or whether it be real derangement, is always in dialogue with others. For example, as Claudius packs him off to England, Hamlet says, "Farewell dear mother." "Your loving father, Hamlet," says his uncle. "My mother," Hamlet replies. "Father and mother is man and wife, man and wife is one flesh, and so my mother." His last barb, masked as random mockery, plays once more upon the technical incestuousness of Claudius's marriage and his own distaste for it.

Ophelia's derangement manifests very differently. She speaks in isolation, in a sort of personal code. She uses fragments of songs about death and sexual betrayal seemingly at random to articulate her fractured self, her torn emotions. I'm always intrigued by the song she sings out of nowhere in Act 4, scene 5. "Tomorrow is Saint Valentine's day, all in the morning betime. And I a maid at your window, to be your Valentine. Then up he rose and donned his clothes, and dupp'd the chamber door. Let in the maid, that out a maid, never departed more." She comes in a virgin; she doesn't leave a virgin. "By Gis and by Saint Charity, alack and fie for shame. Young men will do't if they come to it. By cock they are to blame. Quoth she, before you tumbled me, you promised me to wed. So would I have done, by yonder sun, if thou hadst not come to my bed."

A woman gives her virginity, her maidenhead to her beloved, and then is cast aside. The ballad gives us its own glimpse at the double standard that governs this society. The scorn felt for a woman who acts on her desire, the sense of a world where men both desire women sexually and shrink from women who manifest their sexuality. What's this song doing here? Is this speaking to something in her past with Hamlet? Is she breaking through the role of the maddened bereft daughter in mourning to speak as the betrayed lover?

What's striking about Ophelia's madness is how differently people respond to it. Hamlet's got the whole court on edge. People are always pressing him to find out what he means. Ophelia's madness barely communicates to anybody. She becomes a spectacle that gives people pain and distress, but she's not dangerous, even when she speaks the truth. When Ophelia reappears all in her madness after Laertes has come back to the Danish court, she's holding flowers that she's gathered and she starts to distribute them to Laertes, to

Gertrude, and Claudius. There's a long tradition of different flowers having different symbolic meanings, the so-called language of flowers, and Ophelia is making use of it.

"There's rosemary, that's for remembrance. Pray love, remember. [And] there's pansies, that's for thoughts." She gives rosemary for remembrance and pansies for thoughts to her brother. Remember me, think on me. "There's fennel for you and columbines," she goes on. "There's rue for you and here's some for me… Oh, you must wear your rue with a difference." Fennel and columbines signified respectively, marital infidelity and flattery. Is she addressing Gertrude and Claudius here? And then the mention of the plant rue with the obvious pun on regret. Who gets that rue from her and why must he or she wear it with a difference?

She may be getting some interesting jabs in here, but look what happens. Laertes says, "Thought and affliction, passion, hell itself, she turns to favor and to prettiness." He insists that what we have here is a pathetic yet pretty spectacle, something of aesthetic interest only. Not the kind of madness that speaks dangerous truths. And Ophelia exits from the play still singing her odd little songs. She'll appear again only as a dead body.

Strikingly, it is Gertrude who gets to report Ophelia's death, gets to give her a gentle lyrical tribute. Claudius and Laertes are, after all, too busy plotting how to kill Hamlet to notice what's happening to Ophelia. Their conversation is interrupted by Gertrude bringing her sad news:

> "There is a willow grows aslant a brook, that shows his hoar leaves in the glassy stream. There with fantastic garlands did she make of crow flowers, nettles, daisies, and long purples, that liberal shepherds give a grosser name, but our cold maids do dead men's fingers call them. There on the pendant boughs her crownet weeds clambering to hang, an envious sliver broke, when down her weedy trophies and herself fell in the weeping brook. Her clothes spread wide and, mermaid like, awhile they bore her up, which time she chanted snatches of old tunes, as one incapable of her own distress, or like a creature native and indued unto that element. But long it could not be till that her garments, heavy with their

drink, pulled the poor wretch from her melodious lay to muddy death."

The woman disappears among the flowers and the natural setting. Her only action is to seek to hang her flowers on the willow. There was a longstanding folk-tradition in England that deserted or betrayed lovers hang symbols of their love on weeping willow trees. But, then what? Ophelia barely initiates any more action, an envious sliver broke. Gertrude makes the tree the thing that acts, a malicious branch breaks off. Her clothes bear her up for a while, then heavy with moisture pull her to her death. She isn't in control. She was never in control. Her passivity in the water suggests a kind of will not to survive, but it is hardly the kind of consciously chosen self-slaughter that Hamlet agonizes about at such length.

The very last we will see of Ophelia, to be sure, is the dead body receiving rather rushed burial at the end of the gravedigger scene at the start of Act 5. It seems entirely characteristic that she is, in effect, displaced from her own grave by her brother and by Hamlet himself, when both men almost come to blows in the burial space prepared for her, each of them claiming to have loved her best. But, I shall have more to say about this in my next lecture, as I consider the final scenes of the tragedy.

Lecture Six
Hamlet IV—Uncontainable *Hamlet*

Scope:

Hamlet is at once a sprawling and encyclopedic play and a play full of silences and mysteries. Addressing the difficulty of determining what exactly lies at the center of this play, this lecture offers an account of some resonant moments in its closing stages: the odd revelation of Hamlet's true age in the graveyard scene, the prince's new knowledge that "the readiness is all," and the hero's final request that Horatio safeguard his reputation by telling his story properly to posterity. After discussing the near impossibility of ever containing the multifarious events of the play within a single interpretation, it will consider the interpretive gap that opens up between the "unfoldings" of Hamlet's story voiced by characters *within* the play and the larger understanding of both Hamlet and *Hamlet* available to members of its audience.

Outline

I. *Hamlet* is play that, like its hero, resists interpretation. One can attempt to "pluck out the heart of [its] mystery"; one can also suggest the problems that beset any interpretation that tries to contain its multiplicity.

II. It is possible to offer a summation of the play that begins with the gravedigger scene of Act 5.

    A. In this scene, we learn that Hamlet is 30. Previously, his concerns have been those of someone just entering adulthood, but this information seems to point to a newly mature Hamlet.

    B. The scene suggests that Hamlet's desire for his own death has been transformed into a more general meditation on death as an ending to all actions and all dramas.

    C. This suggests that he has achieved some distance on the questions that have been lacerating him.

III. This larger vision of life is also evident in the action preceding the duel with Laertes.

A. Hamlet speaks of a "divinity that shapes our ends" and seems to accept that life may, after all, have some significant design to it (in contrast to his former insistence on its meaninglessness).

B. Hamlet evinces a renewed confidence in his power to act forcefully, describing how he foiled Claudius's plot against his life.

C. Hamlet offers a justification of revenge, redefining the killing of Claudius as a healing action that can be morally justified.

D. Although he has some misgivings before the fencing match with Laertes, Hamlet reasserts his belief in a providential design and surrenders his will to a higher destiny.

IV. Hamlet's change of heart seems to be justified, after a fashion, in what ensues.

A. He achieves revenge without, precisely, initiating murder.

B. His actions are publicly justified by Laertes's revelations about Claudius's murderous plots.

C. Hamlet dies commanding Horatio to tell the story that will preserve his honor after death.

D. He is able to name Fortinbras as his successor.

V. The above account is nevertheless only *one* story that might be told about *Hamlet*.

A. All accounts of *Hamlet* and all performances of it (most directors cut the long play-text) are only partial versions of the drama.

B. The design of the play raises the question of whether it is indeed a revenge tragedy or, rather, a play *about* revenge tragedies.

C. Given the play's capaciousness and its canvassing of so many topics, it is hard to tell what is central to the action and what is a digression from that center.

VI. There are parts of the play that cannot easily be contained by the account given above, and the ending raises as many questions as it resolves.

A. The disturbing confrontation between Laertes and Hamlet over Ophelia's dead body begs the question of whether the love Hamlet now claims to have felt for Ophelia is supported by his behavior elsewhere in the play.

B. When Hamlet apologizes to Laertes before the fencing match, he blames the killing of Polonius on his madness. Is he evading responsibility for his single most problematic action?

C. Hamlet's request that Horatio tell his story properly invites us to ask what would constitute an adequate report. Horatio's subsequent summary of events does not reaffirm his friend's declaration that there is a providential destiny that shapes our ends.

D. Although Hamlet designated Fortinbras his successor, Fortinbras swiftly seizes the throne of Denmark *without* Horatio telling him of Hamlet's decree.

E. The soldier's burial Fortinbras gives to Hamlet seems to offer a somewhat inappropriate end to a very complicated story.

VII. It may be a characteristic of Shakespearean tragedy that the complexities of the experience it seeks to represent escape those who speak the official final words of a play.

A. In older forms of tragedy, a chorus of speakers who had observed the action but were not entangled in it would offer a summation or draw a moral—but there is no chorus in Hamlet.

B. The reader or spectator of this play must be an active interpreter of its intricate action if he or she is to do a better job of unfolding Hamlet's story than either Horatio or Fortinbras.

Essential Reading:

Shakespeare, *Hamlet.*

Supplementary Reading/Viewing:

Booth, "On the Value of Hamlet," in *Shakespeare: An Anthology of Criticism and Theory, 1945–2000*, Russ McDonald, ed., pp. 225–244.

One or more of the film versions of *Hamlet* directed by Olivier, Zeffirelli, and Branagh (all available on VHS and DVD).

Questions to Consider:

1. Take a look at the last scene of *Hamlet* in the movies directed by Zeffirelli and Olivier. What are the most interesting differences between the directors' interpretations of the play's conclusion? Which version do you find most attractive—and why?

2. Is Hamlet a man who is sometimes truly deranged or a man whose madness is always and only pretended? What difference might your opinion make to your overall interpretation of this tragedy?

Lecture Six—Transcript
Hamlet IV—Uncontainable *Hamlet*

Towards the end of Act 3, scene 2 of *Hamlet*, the after-dinner entertainment from hell has caused Claudius to flee the room and the court to disperse in disarray. It's at this point that Rosencrantz and Guildenstern, those supremely incompetent surveillance specialists, show up to tell Hamlet that Claudius is furious with him, his mother wants to see him immediately, and to ask him once more just why he's acting so weirdly. Hamlet doesn't answer them directly, but, instead, gives Guildenstern a music lesson, courtesy of one of the players who has just shown up carrying a recorder. The prince invites Guildenstern to play upon the pipe, and when Guildenstern protests that he does not have the skill, Hamlet declares:

> "Why, look you now, how unworthy a thing you make of me. You would play upon me. You would seem to know my stops. You would pluck out the heart of my mystery. You would sound me from my lowest note to the top of my compass and there is much music, excellent voice in this little organ, yet cannot you make it speak. 'Sblood, do you think I'm easier to be played on than a pipe? Call me what instrument you will, though you can fret me, you cannot play upon me."

Hamlet's accusation that Rosencrantz and Guildenstern are attempting an impossible thing in seeking to pluck out the "heart of his mystery" echoes his declaration to Gertrude that he has "that within that passeth show." His insistence that they can't find out the inner music that moves him, that his true self is ultimately inaccessible to them is for me one of the most telling moments of this play. In some sense, we're in the same position as the hapless Rosencrantz and Guildenstern. We are trying to try to find the heart of the mystery not just of Hamlet the prince, but of *Hamlet* the tragic drama.

I want to do two things in this lecture. I am first going to give an interpretation of the end of the play, which will offer one way of untangling its mysteries. I'm then going to suggest some of the limitations and problems that beset any attempt to offer an interpretation, which completely contains or sorts out the complicated action of *Hamlet*.

First, let me go off on a slight tangent. How old is prince Hamlet? We aren't actually told this until very near the end of the play. In the scene with the gravedigger, when Hamlet asks the sardonic fellow how long he's been digging graves, he's told that the gravedigger entered his profession the day young Hamlet was born. The man then adds, "I have been sexton here, man and boy, thirty years." This information often surprises careful readers. In Act 1, Hamlet is called young Hamlet and his concerns seem very much those of somebody just entering into adulthood, trying to establish an identity of his own, rebelling against parent figures who seem to want to control his life, dealing with problems to do with his own sexuality and that of others, meditating obsessively on what it all means, why am I here, what's the point of it all, not to mention dressing in black a lot and being sarcastic.

And then, we learn he's 30. This belated knowledge has, I'd suggest, poetic rather than logical significance. He can't really be 20 in Act 1 and 30 in Act 5. But, at least one critic has suggested that Shakespeare, rather than forgetting what he's up to, may be drawing our attention to the fact that the Hamlet who returns to the court in Act 5 from his aborted voyage to England is, in effect, a different man, a more mature hero. Let's explore this notion.

We first meet Hamlet on his return in a graveyard, which seems suitable enough since he has been talking about death ever since his very first soliloquy. We've previously heard him wishing that his "too, too solid flesh" would melt or discussing the fears of what may come after death, the fears that "make us rather bear those ills we have than fly to others which we know not of." Now, however, he speaks of death in more general terms, putting the actions he may or may not carry out in a larger perspective. Hamlet and Horatio watch the gravedigger at his task. Even as he digs the new grave, he is turning over the remains of people who have died before. Hamlet observes that nothing these poor skeletons did while alive has saved them from the grave. All the cases, the deceptive gambits and tricks of the lawyer, all the witty pranks of the court jester, could not hold off death. The court lady could not disguise the inevitable decay of her flesh with all her cosmetics, even if she painted them on an inch thick.

Death, too, is the great equalizer. You can't tell the difference between a king's skeleton and a peasant's. And as their bodies gradually turn to dust, there are no heroes in the bone yard. One rotting corpse looks very much like another. Hamlet asks, "Dost thou think Alexander looked of this fashion in the earth?" He means, of course, Alexander the Great, the Greek ruler and general who, at a ridiculously young age, conquered vast territories of Asia Minor and supposedly wept that there were no more worlds to conquer. Hamlet goes on to imagine how even the body of a hero and a warlord returning to the earth will eventually become part of the clay used to stop up a bunghole in a beer barrel. Ashes to ashes, dust to dust.

All our dramas have the same end. All our actions, however heroic, come to this, he's saying. This larger perspective suggests a Hamlet who's got some distance from the things that were lacerating him earlier. And you might also note, he has no more soliloquies in Act 5. A soliloquy is a verbal space where somebody explores the conflicts within himself. Does this mean that Hamlet is no longer a divided and tormented individual?

We see this larger perspective again at the start of the next scene, when Hamlet tells Horatio how he escaped Claudius's plotting. Following a hunch, he examined the letters his escorts, Rosencrantz and Guildenstern, were taking to the English King, and discovered an order for his execution, which he then replaced with an order for their execution. As he starts to describe the events that led to the letter substitution, he says, "There's a divinity"—a deity—"that shapes our ends. Rough hew them how we will." In context, he seems to mean that a larger force has gone about saving him. The metaphor is an interesting one. Hamlet offers the notion of a god who is a kind of sculptor, as opposed to a mere woodchopper roughly hewing his materials. He seems to suggest that God, the artist, has shaped a universe with some meaningful patterns to it after all. Humanity is subject to a shaping destiny rather than mere chance, or rather than its own fumbling, clumsy efforts to bring order out of chaos. We should perhaps also notice the pun on ends. That divinity shapes our ends in the sense of our aims, our goals, and also the way we end, the way we die. It seems that Hamlet is no longer in rebellion against weary, flat, stale, unprofitable life, but accepts that it might, after all, have a meaningful design to it.

As he describes how he himself reshaped Claudius's plot and turned it onto Rosencrantz and Guildenstern, he mentions that he had in his possession his own father's signet ring, the sign of royal authority.

Using it to seal the letter he has rewritten, he gets to act as king at last. He displaces Claudius, Claudius who had usurped the place of his father. Indeed, he now seems to speak from a position of royal confidence. When Horatio notes, rather queasily, that Rosencrantz and Guildenstern have been sent to their deaths in England, Hamlet says, "They are not near my conscience. Their defeat doth by their own insinuation grow." Their willingness to be used against me brought about their destruction. And he adds that men ought to look out when they get caught up in battles between more powerful opponents. Horatio exclaims, "Why, what a king is this!" Is Hamlet, indeed, claiming his own regal identity at last? Horatio seems to think so.

The exchange with Horatio ends with Hamlet offering a new summary of the evidence justifying his taking action against Claudius. Don't you think, he says, that given what Claudius has done, "he that hath killed my king and whored my mother, popped in between the election and my hopes, thrown out his angle for my proper life, and with such cozenage, is it not perfect conscience to quit him with this arm? And is it not to be damned to let this canker of our nature come in further evil?"

He seems to have solved the problem of the conscience that makes cowards of us all. He does not say now, will I be damned if I do murder at the ghost's bidding? But, rather, he asks will I not be damned if I let the canker, the cancerous disease, the rot, spread further? Is it not an act of true moral conscience to kill Claudius?

His question never gets answered by Horatio and, in fact, doesn't have to be. Hamlet doesn't have to plot any more about what to do with Claudius because another plot is closing in on him. For, now, the preening courtier Osric arrives bearing a challenge from Laertes to a supposedly friendly fencing match. Hamlet has no conscious suspicion that this is a setup job, but he does have a moment of foreboding. Horatio jokingly teases him that he'll lose the wager. I do not think so, says Hamlet. "Since he went into France, I have been in continual practice. I shall win at the odds. But thou wouldst not think how ill all's here about my heart." Horatio picks up on this moment of uncertainty. "If your mind dislike anything, obey it." But, Hamlet refuses to refuse the fight. "We defy augury," he says. We scorn mysterious prophetic fears about the future. He continues: "There's a special providence in the fall of a sparrow. If it be now, 'tis not to come. If it be not to come, it will be now. If it be not now, yet it will come. The readiness is all." The "it," of course, is death.

This special providence that shapes our ends and includes even so small a thing as a sparrow's death—Hamlet is not talking about fate, a pre-Christian notion of actions pre-ordained by uncaring cosmic forces, nor is he talking about the malicious caprices of the goddess Fortune. He's once more offering a Christian an optimistic belief in a higher design. If he dies now, there will be a reason behind that death. It will have its place in the divinity's larger plans. And, indeed, when he surrenders his will to a higher scheme of things, providence does seem to step in, after a fashion. Through the accidental reversals of the duel, the exchange of swords that occurs in the heat of action, he is given the chance of achieving revenge without precisely initiating murder. Laertes, poisoned with his own poisoned weapon, is struck by conscience and reveals Claudius's plots before he dies. And Claudius's plots have already turned back on themselves. The king's treacherous backup plan to poison the wine he offers Hamlet leads instead to the death of his beloved Gertrude.

By the time Hamlet actually stabs Claudius and forces him to finish the wine, the whole court knows Claudius is a traitor and murderer receiving his deserved punishment. Laertes forgives Hamlet for his father's death and in saying "Exchange forgiveness with me, noble Hamlet," publicly reaffirms the prince's integrity.

Hamlet dies, but he's ensured that Horatio will tell the story that will preserve his honor after his death. Young Hamlet has taken over old Hamlet's role. He's now the one saying remember me. And he even gets to name his successor before he dies. This is Fortinbras, whose words conclude the play. Fortinbras pays tribute to the dead prince and promises him a warrior's burial.

So, I've finished off *Hamlet*, but I haven't finished. To be honest, I'm only partly satisfied with this account of the ending of the play. It's a bit too glib, a bit too pat. This play perpetually eludes my control. At the beginning of the Olivier movie version, we hear a voiceover portentously announcing, "This is the story of a man who could not make up his mind." Well, that's one story to be found in *Hamlet*. But as I've previously mentioned, productions of *Hamlet* tend to be partial versions of the play. It's so long that directors almost always make cuts in the script. Olivier, for example, omits Fortinbras, Rosencrantz and Guildenstern, and most of Hamlet's conversations with the players from his version.

To omit bits of a text is as much an act of reinterpretation as rewriting it directly. And even when we read the whole text, we nearly always end up constructing a selective narrative of its action and its themes in our minds. I've already mentioned that the action of this play includes shadowy reflections and refractions of Hamlet's own story in those of Laertes and Fortinbras who are involved in their own revenge plots. Shakespeare's juxtaposition of these characters with a hero who meditates on his actions almost every step of the way and insists on looking towards their possible results potentially turns the play into a critique of the whole idea of revenge tragedy. It's not so much a revenge tragedy, as a play about revenge tragedies.

It's also a hugely encyclopedic play. Remember that long list I gave you in my last lecture of all the issues that it takes on board. It's extraordinarily difficult to work out what is at the center of *Hamlet* and what is a digression from its main themes. One might ask, for example, are the prince's meditations on the meaning of life and death digressions from the revenge plot? Or is the revenge plot merely the occasion, the pretext, for his existential meditations, which are the real heart of the play?

I used Hamlet's apparent surrender to the providence that he now seems to find in even so small a thing as the fall of a sparrow to focus the ending of the play, suggesting that when Hamlet defers to a higher scheme of things, he's rewarded with a noble ending and a meaningful death. But, there are parts of the play that are never quite resolved by the ending I traced and that ending itself opens matters out again in teasing ways. I want to look first at a couple of things that, for me at least, don't ever get properly subordinated to or re-explained by the ending.

First, the incredibly disturbing and competitive confrontation between Laertes and Hamlet at Ophelia's grave at end of Act 5, scene 1. When both of them leap into her grave shouting, the episode threatens to devolve into a crude competition over who loved her best. As they rave over her corpse, two men who have bullied her in life, now literally trample her in death. Hamlet insists, "I loved

Ophelia. Forty thousand brothers could not, with all their quantity of love, make up my sum." So, what are we to make of Hamlet's insisting he loved Ophelia so much better than Laertes? He hasn't previously said one word about his feelings for Ophelia to any third party. Nor does he refer to her in any of the early soliloquies, which lay out his misery. And he never says anything that suggests he has recognized that he might be responsible for her fate, that the combination of his cruelty to her and his murder of her father might have pushed her over the edge. Is he just theatricalizing his grief here? Has his demonstration of his sorrow simply become the occasion to reassert his own identity? "This is I, Hamlet the Dane," he says, as he jumps into her grave.

I'm also made uneasy by Hamlet's speech to Laertes before they fight their duel. Formally asking his pardon and referring back to the slaying of Polonius, Hamlet says:

> "What I have done that might your nature, honor, and exception roughly awake, I here proclaim was madness. Was it Hamlet wronged Laertes? Never Hamlet. If Hamlet from himself be taken away and when he's not himself does wrong Laertes, then Hamlet does it not. Hamlet denies it. Who does it then? His madness. If it be so, Hamlet is of the faction that is wronged; his madness is poor Hamlet's enemy."

The speech re-complicates the issue of moral agency. Hamlet has, after all, killed Laertes's father and been the indirect cause of his sister's madness and possible suicide. By invoking his supposed madness as his excuse, is Hamlet just using a clever rationalization? Or, is he now claiming the antic disposition was, in fact, a reality, looking back on his actions and realizing he was deranged, making the insanity plea. What he says here contradicts what he said during his confrontation with Gertrude in her bedchamber, that she must not deceive herself, that it was his madness speaking when he berated her for her actions. Here, the prince speaks of a deranged Hamlet who did that bad stuff when he was not himself. Hamlets don't kill people, madness kills people. But was he mad when he killed Polonius, given that in that scene he had made it clear he thought it was the hated Claudius behind the arras? Might this gracefully apologetic Hamlet, in fact be Hamlet at his nearest to Claudius, the good politician ready with a glib excuse? Hamlet, the spin-doctor?

And finally, there's the matter of the ending of this play, which raises its own questions. On the point of death, Hamlet addresses the horrified onlookers. "I am dead, Horatio. Wretched queen, adieu. You that look pale and tremble at this chance, that are but mutes or audience to this act, had I but time, oh I could tell you, but let it be." Note the way his language suggests that what has just happened was, in some sense, a theatrical performance in which the dazed courtiers are the mutes—that is, the extras. It is as if Hamlet, having triumphed over other people's plots, now stages himself on his own terms and once again by way of a story that doesn't get told, that "passeth show." "O I could tell you..."—he sounds like the ghost.

Hamlet begs Horatio to "report me and my cause aright to the unsatisfied —to do what is necessary to prevent Hamlet leaving what he calls a "wounded name" behind him in this world, to see to his reputation by unfolding him properly. I'm invoking that word from the very beginning of the play and, in a sense, we are back where we started. The opening began with a command to stand and unfold yourself. Now, Hamlet wants himself unfolded by Horatio.

But this raises the question of what it means to report Hamlet aright, what his story is. Is it the tale of a man who could not make up his mind? Is it the story of a noble revenger who did his duty at the last? Is it the story of somebody who was tempted to revenge, who finally realized that vengeance belongs to God, not man? Is it the story of a sensitive scholar who was placed in a situation where the very qualities that made him superior to other people, his capacity to love strongly, his powers of introspection, made him particularly vulnerable and at once ineffective and deadly dangerous?

Well, Horatio does tell Hamlet's story, sort of. Horatio begins the play as the witness invited to authenticate the sentries' vision of a dead man. He ends the play bearing witness for the dead man's son. Speaking to Fortinbras, as they both stand among the dead bodies, Horatio says that he will unfold "how these things came about. So shall you hear of carnal, bloody and unnatural acts, of accidental judgments, casual slaughters, of purposes mistook fallen on the inventors' heads. All this I can truly deliver." He speaks of accident and chance and destructive actions, which turn back upon the heads of their inventors. He doesn't speak of providence, or a sense of a larger significant design—that is, Horatio does not reaffirm Hamlet's assertion that there is a providential destiny that shapes our ends.

We might want to ask, what are the implications of Fortinbras, the man of action who has been hovering threateningly on the margins of events throughout, ending up the inheritor of Denmark? He says, "I have some rights of memory in this kingdom," but never explains what these rights are. And, although Hamlet designated Fortinbras his successor, Fortinbras in fact declares himself king without Horatio telling him of Hamlet's casting vote. I have, in fact, seen at least one performance of the end of this play in which Fortinbras's arrival is much more like an invasion, a coup d'état. And the last thing you see is Horatio being beaten and dragged off by his soldiers. At any rate, Fortinbras inherits. Is pure unthinking will to action left triumphant at the last?

Fortinbras claims that if Hamlet had been put on, put on the throne, put to the test, he was, says Fortinbras, likely to have proved most royally, to have shown himself to be a true king, which seems to echo Horatio's earlier "Why, what a king is this!" But, one wonders just what would be Fortinbras's definition of "most royal"? Is the soldier's burial he gives Hamlet the true end of the man we've seen, or are we seeing a sort of pasted on conventional ending to a much more complicated story? At the end of Shakespearean tragedies, the survivors, usually by definition not the central characters, get to say the last words. But, their vision of what has occurred or their summing up of the dead hero, is likely to be a partial and incomplete one. And on the other hand, it may be a characteristic of tragedy itself that not everything will be fully articulated in its action, that the tragic experience escapes the words of the figures within the play.

In the tragedy of ancient Greece, the last words are given to the chorus, a group of bystanders who have watched the action throughout and who then attempt some kind of summation of its significance. But, there's no chorus in *Hamlet*, which means that if readers or audiences of this play want to grasp the action whole, they are going to have to think for themselves and ask themselves whether they can do a better job of unfolding Hamlet's story than either Horatio or Fortinbras.

Lecture Seven
Othello I—Miscegenation and Mixed Messages

Scope:

This lecture begins with a discussion of Renaissance notions of race and cultural geography; it then glances at the semantic slippage, in Shakespeare's play, between the material differences of black and white skin and the metaphysical connotations of the black/white opposition. It explores just what it means to call Othello a "Moor" and examines the contrast between the way he is presented in Iago's abusive exchange with Desdemona's father and the way his own language constructs his identity. Analyzing in some detail Othello and Desdemona's defense of their love before the Venetian Senate, it considers Shakespeare's highly nuanced treatment of Desdemona's "errant" marriage. The lecture concludes by addressing the self-division evident in Othello's uneasy negotiation of his double identity as warrior and lover.

Outline

I. Othello is a North African "Moor" leading Venetian forces against the Turks of the Ottoman Empire in defense of the Venetian colony of Cyprus: his tragedy has a complex social geography.

   A. The city-state of Venice was a rich trading center. Italians were generally associated by the English with political intrigue and savage vendettas; Venice was also remarkable for its expensive prostitutes.

   B. The Muslim Turks, who threaten Cyprus, were considered pagan enemies by western Europeans.

   C. Othello is himself an alien of sorts: despite his Christianity, his blackness makes him an exotic "other" to the Venetians. He is admired as a warrior, but his marriage to Desdemona appalls her father.

   D. The Turkish threat that starts out the play is soon dispelled; the play's disputed territory shifts from the island of Cyprus to the body of Desdemona.

II. Our first acquaintance with Othello comes by way of the secret slanders of Iago and the increasingly hysterical response of Brabantio.

    A. Iago and his "gull," Roderigo, play upon 16th-century racial stereotypes in characterizing Othello as both bestial and demonic.

    B. Brabantio assumes that his daughter's "unnatural" action in marrying Othello must mean that she is the victim of some form of black magic.

    C. A dualistic mode of thought in which black and white skins are equated with evil and virtue, respectively, is reinforced by the men's words; the play will proceed to complicate these tidy oppositions when Iago's evil blackens the whiteness of Desdemona.

III. Othello's first appearance on stage allows us to compare him with Iago's slanderous portrait.

    A. Othello speaks with absolute self-possession and dignity and assumes that his merits will speak for themselves.

    B. He refuses to be drawn into violence by Brabantio and the mob who threaten him, and his behavior offers a striking contrast to Brabantio's hysterical speeches.

IV. When Othello and Desdemona defend their actions before the Venetian senate, their marriage is ratified—but the scene hints at problems to come.

    A. Brabantio insists upon the "unnatural" nature of Desdemona's love for Othello and suggests that if she has deceived her father, she may deceive her husband.

    B. The marriage that testifies to Desdemona's love for Othello is not viewed as an admirable transcendence of prejudice by Brabantio, who redefines it as an act of female transgression and social disobedience.

    C. Othello offers a passionate and persuasive account of his wooing of Desdemona that nevertheless amplifies earlier intimations that his marriage is a cause of anxiety.

        1. He has previously associated entering into marriage with a circumscription of his identity and a restriction upon his freedom of movement.

2. His description of why he loves Desdemona focuses exclusively on his utter investment in Desdemona's love for him.

D. When Desdemona frankly insists that she wishes to accompany Othello to Cyprus (and consummate her marriage), Othello supports her plea more cautiously, insisting that her presence will not detract from his warrior identity.

V. Othello exhibits a certain self-division: his notion of himself as warrior-leader seems at odds with his imagination of himself as Desdemona's husband. This will make him particularly vulnerable to Iago's manipulations.

Essential Reading:

Shakespeare, *Othello*.

Supplementary Reading:

Snyder, *The Comic Matrix of Shakespeare's Tragedies*, pp. 73–90.

Questions to Consider:

1. To what extent does the language that Shakespeare gives Othello differentiate him from other characters in the first act of the play? Does his style of speech indeed present him as significantly "other" in the world of Venice?

2. Desdemona says, "I saw Othello's visage in his mind"; the Duke tells Brabantio, "If virtue no delighted beauty lack, / Your son-in-law is far more fair than black." What do they mean by these speeches and are they, in fact, saying the same thing?

Lecture Seven—Transcript
Othello I—Miscegenation and Mixed Messages

I'll start with a confession. Of all Shakespeare's tragedies, I find *Othello* the most unbearable to watch. It has a certain claustrophobic horror. The play starts with the suggestion it's going to be concerned with international conflict, but it swiftly narrows to the doings of a very few characters in an intimately domestic setting, as a new marriage is torn apart by poisonous jealousy. We watch, helplessly, the insidious corruption of a warrior's mind and the destruction of a generous-hearted woman. We watch a horribly creative evildoer wreak havoc on other people's lives until we're left staring at three broken bodies on a bed. The play begins where many comedies end. Two lovers overcome social obstacles and are united in marriage. But, Shakespeare writes beyond the end of comedy, taking us into very dark territory, indeed.

The first act of *Othello* takes place in Venice, Italy, the remainder in Cyprus. Here are a few preliminary words about the social geography of *Othello*. A 17th-century English audience would bring their own preconceptions to a play in which most of the characters are Italians. Italy was a land associated in the popular mind with learning and the arts, but also with political intrigue, with savage vendettas and the art of the duel, and with assassination and poison. At this time, Italy was not a unified country, but an agglomeration of independent city-states, often warring with one another and often hiring foreign mercenaries to fight for them. Venice was one of these city-states, a great port and a particularly rich trading center, ruled by sophisticated merchant princes. Shakespeare had already visited it in his rather dark comedy, *The Merchant of Venice*. Venice was highly cosmopolitan. You'd meet citizens of many other countries trading there and it was infamous, or famous, for its expensive and beautiful high class prostitutes, its courtesans. But, most of this play doesn't take place in Venice, but in Cyprus, a large island in the eastern Mediterranean near Turkey, which has always been disputed territory. In the play, it's ruled by Venice, but threatened by the Turks of the powerful Muslim Ottoman Empire, who are perceived by the Europeans as pagan barbarians. So, we have an outpost of a Christian empire, which is threatened by enemy aliens. And we quickly learn that its chief defender, the general of the Venetian forces is himself, an alien, a foreigner, a North African, a Christian moor, Othello.

I should speak a little bit first about that term *moor*, which is rather vaguely used at the time Shakespeare was writing to refer to not just an inhabitant of Morocco, but any African, whether Arab or Black. The play makes it clear, however, that Othello is a black man; Iago brutally derides its hero's African features. For early 17th-century audiences, the word moor conjures up a certain exoticism, something dangerous, something emphatically other, not necessarily a person to be enslaved. Although John Hawkins had taken a first boatload of Africans to the Americas about 40 years previously, the transatlantic slave trade hadn't really yet got underway.

Incidentally, Londoners would have been used to seeing black Africans. They would have come to the city as sailors on trading ships, for example, and some of them appear to have settled there. Indeed, in 1596, Queen Elizabeth I writes a letter to the lord mayor of London expressing concern at the large number of what she calls blackamoors in the city and suggesting that they be encouraged to leave.

In this play, Othello has a foot in two cultural camps. He is perceived as a respected warrior, who is absolutely essential to Venice's security. He's valiant Othello. But, he's also an alien. We learn that Brabanzio has invited him to his house, honoring him as a noble employee of the Venetian state. But, Brabanzio is appalled when he discovers that his daughter has married this same noble soldier.

Although Act 1 is pervaded with anxiety about the Turkish threat, and Act 1, scene 3 starts with a series of contradictory messages about the destination of the Turkish fleet, the military crisis is resolved by the end of Act 2, scene 1, with the news of the dispersal and wreck of the Turkish fleet and the safe arrival of Othello's forces in Cyprus. The rest of the play will take place in this imaginative Cyprus space, halfway between ostensibly civilized Venice and the territory of threatening otherness. But, the disputed territory will not be Cyprus itself. Instead, two other disputed territories are at issue in the action. One is a woman's body, Desdemona's, which Iago and Roderigo initially represent in the crudest terms as being invaded and stolen by an alien. The other disputed territory is the mind and soul of Othello, which Iago is determined to poison and corrupt. The play starts with the suggestion of a broad political context for the character's actions, but the center of action gradually narrows into the domestic sphere, and it will climax in the most intimate space imaginable, the marriage bed of Othello and Desdemona.

Shakespeare delays Othello's first entrance. Before we meet the moor, himself, we have heard other characters speak forcibly about him. His identity has been constructed by the slanders of Iago, his duplicitous "ancient" or ensign, and by Roderigo, Desdemona's disappointed suitor. And we've watched Brabanzio, Desdemona's father, transform Othello into a kind of evil magician. I'm going to be talking at some length about Iago's poisonous use of language in my next lecture. For the moment, I'm going to focus on Brabanzio's response to the news his daughter has eloped with Othello. Shrouded in darkness, working with Roderigo to drive Brabanzio into violent action, Iago shouts up at the senator's window. "Even now, now, very now, an old black ram is tupping your white ewe. Arise! Arise! Or else the devil will make a grandsire of you."

He speaks of Desdemona being covered with a Barbary horse. He describes Othello and Desdemona as making the beast with two backs. Roderigo helpfully adds that she lies in the gross clasps of a lascivious moor. They create a vision of the sexual union of Othello and Desdemona that reduces it to animals rutting.

The plotters are manipulating those nastier bits of Brabanzio's mind that might be tempted to think of a black man as something bestial or even as something demonic, for in popular belief, the devil was depicted as black. And Brabanzio responds to Iago's slanderous manipulation just as Iago would wish. His hysteria is the more striking because we will learn from Othello himself that Brabanzio had often invited Othello to his house, had let him speak alone with Desdemona, had treated him as a noble warrior worthy of all hospitality, for it had never crossed Brabanzio's mind that Othello could possibly be a sexual threat to his daughter. We know Brabanzio had considered Roderigo unworthy of Desdemona. He starts the exchange with Roderigo repeating that the man will never get to marry his daughter. But, by the time that Iago, lurking in the darkness, has finished with him, Brabanzio is saying he'd rather have had this idiot married to Desdemona than the noble general, Othello. Indeed, the situation seems so unnatural to him that this sophisticated, civilized Venetian senator can only imagine that

Othello has used black magic to win his daughter. "Is there not charms by which the property of youth and maid hood, may be abused? Have you not read, Roderigo, of some such thing?"

Notice how deeply embedded the cultural assumptions are in all of this. The easy slippage between blackness and evil, black skin and black deeds, black magic. The Western world has always liked to think in tidy dualities, diagramming things so that Black, evil, ugly line up on one side and White, fair, virtuous, beautiful on the other. Brabanzio finds it easy to think of a black man as a black magician. But Shakespeare, having put an apparent embodiment of utter opposites—a black man, a white woman—at the center of his play, then goes on to complicate all the easy dualities. It's Iago, the white man, who is the morally blackened man and his particular evil will be to transform the noble black man from a generous loving husband to a monster of jealousy. And he'll do this by making Othello think that the white skin of his aristocratic bride is just a deceiving mask for her dark and corrupt soul.

To return to the start of the play, by the end of Act 1, scene 1, Othello has been labeled and constructed in various unpleasant ways—as a black ram, a devil, a trickster, a thief, a black magician. But then, we actually get to see him for ourselves in the next scene. Iago, slipping away from the mischief he's caused to rejoin his superior officer, pretends deep concern for the risk presented by Brabanzio. He asks Othello if he is firmly married because the enraged father is likely to try to divorce him from Desdemona and is all set to work his vengeance on him. This is Othello's response: "Let him do his spite. My services which I have done the signory shall out tongue his complaints. 'Tis yet to know which when I know that boasting is an honor, I shall promulgate. I fetch my life and being from men of royal siege, and my demerits may speak unbonneted."

Now we actually get a sense of the person who the speakers in Act 1, scene 1 have demonized. We see Othello's absolute self-possession and quiet dignity. He puts it on the record that what he has done for Venice has earned him favors from its ruling class and that his worth must surely outweigh the accusations made against him. He also notes that he is of as high rank as Desdemona. "I fetch my life and being," he says, "from men of royal descent." But, at the same time, he implies that he finds boasting dishonorable and thus has never made much noise about this. His merits will speak for themselves.

When Brabanzio and a mob of his followers come seeking him, Othello stands firm. He rejects Iago's suggestion that he make himself scarce: "I must be found. My parts, my title, my perfect soul shall manifest me rightly." His personal qualities, his rank, his clear conscience will speak for him. When Brabanzio and his men come at him with their weapons drawn, Othello simply says, "Keep up your bright swords, for the dew will rust them." Put away your swords, I'm not going to fight. And the only bloodstains they're going to get here will be from the dew that rusts the metal. It's a wonderful throwaway, elegant line. He's quietly joking in the face of an armed mob and also suggesting that there is nothing that deserves fighting over here.

His self-command stands in striking contrast to Brabanzio's own speeches, when the old man continues to accuse him hysterically of corrupting or seducing Desdemona with black magic or drugs. Othello is calmly prepared to answer for his actions and, of course, he does so at the meeting of the Venetian senate, which follows.

In the scene before the senate, Othello and Desdemona both nobly defend their feelings for one another and their actions. The duke of Venice approves their marriage. Brabanzio grudgingly accepts the match and Desdemona gives further testimony of her love for Othello by refusing to be left behind when he sails to Cyprus. A happy ending, but, unfortunately, we still have four acts to go, so that what it is is rather like a premature end of a Shakespearean comedy. And, even now, there are some undercurrents in this scene, which are worth discussing. For a start, there's Brabanzio's repeated insistence on the unnaturalness of his daughter's behavior. "A maiden never bold, of spirit so still and quiet that her motion blushed at itself. And she in spite of nature, of years, of country, credit, everything, to fall in love with what she feared to look on." To act "against all rules of nature," he argues, a virtuous and gently behaved woman like Desdemona must have been conjured to it by the dark arts.

Now, to be sure, the idea of natural behavior is a very slippery matter. The people in power in any given culture or society tend to have the privilege of deciding what is natural and what is not. Think of all the supposedly scientific writing in the 19th century that ostensibly proved that women were naturally unsuited for taking part in public life or that the dark races were naturally inferior to Caucasians. Brabanzio, at any rate, is utterly unable to contemplate the possibility that his daughter has loved Othello, chosen him of her own free will. Her action, for him, is deeply unnatural. If she wasn't won by trickery or magic, if she really chose the moor for her husband, it can only be symptomatic, he later claims, of something deeply flawed in her character. When he is obliged to let her marriage with Othello stand, he offers this parting shot: "Look to her, moor, if thou hast eyes to see, she has deceived her father and may thee." These lines are going to echo through the play.

There is, of course, some deep illogic here. Brabanzio equates the transgression of Desdemona's deceit in choosing Othello and not letting her father see her love for Othello with a very different transgression, that of sexually betraying her husband. The very act which shows Desdemona's love for Othello is paradoxically interpreted as a sign that she mustn't be trusted to keep faith with Othello. And we should perhaps note the doubleness with which Desdemona's action can be interpreted. On the one hand, she may be seen as a woman who has risen above the arbitrary prejudices of her society to follow her heart, but from Brabanzio's perspective, there's no admirable transcendence of prejudice, only social transgression. To embrace his logic is to assert that Desdemona is a woman who, having broken the rules once, may continue to do so—indeed, is more likely to do so—which makes it all the more interesting that Desdemona herself, when her father confronts her with her deed, is extremely careful to relocate her supposed transgression within the rules of her society. When Desdemona is brought before the senate, Brabanzio asks her, "Where in all this company do you owe most obedience?" and this is her response:

> "My noble father, I do perceive here a divided duty. To you I am bound for life and education... You are the lord of duty. I am hitherto your daughter. But here's my husband and so much duty as my mother showed to you, preferring you before her father, so much I challenge that I may profess due to the moor, my lord."

She insists that she's not a disobedient woman. She has changed masters, as all women must do when they marry in a society which does not offer them an autonomous identity under the law, and in which the church insists on a wife's obedience and submission to her husband. Desdemona suggests that her allegiance must now be to her new lord, just as her mother's was given to Brabanzio when she left her father's house. And of course, we have a faint contemporary survival of this in the marriage ceremony, where the father ritually gives the bride to the husband. Desdemona is perhaps slightly fudging the fact that she has married without formally seeking her father's permission, but she seems to be going out of her way to insist that what she has done is no transgression.

Othello himself in this scene offers his own refutation of the accusation he's used drugs or sorcery to win Desdemona. He modestly assures the senate that he's just a plain soldier who will offer them a "round unvarnished tale," no fancy spin doctoring. It's a story, which he then gives at some considerable length. Is it a "round unvarnished tale"? The duke of Venice responds, "I think this tale would win my daughter too." Othello has his own verbal magic at the start of the play. Here he narrates the history of his wooing and he isn't just plain, he's persuasive and powerful, as he touches upon the stories he told Desdemona of his own action-packed and often agonizing past, and then speaks of her response. "She swore in faith was strange, was passing strange, was pitiful, was wondrous pitiful, she wished she had not heard it, yet she wished that heaven had made her such a man. She thanked me and bade me, if I had a friend that loved her, I should but teach him how to tell my story and that would woo her. Upon this hint I spoke. She loved me for the dangers I had passed, and I loved her that she did pity them. This only is the witchcraft I have used." Othello offers no plain tale. He speaks for himself persuasively and powerfully, as he argues he hasn't seduced Desdemona by sorcery, by dark spells, but has won her by another kind of magic—the stories he related that first won her empathy and then her love.

I'd like now to look a little closer at the information we're given in Act 1 about the nature of Desdemona and Othello's love and especially in relation to Othello's feelings and assumptions about love and marriage. This is structurally important in the play because it is the material Iago will have to work with as he pursues his plotting in subsequent acts.

Before we even meet Desdemona, Othello offers some suggestive opinions about marriage in his brief exchange with Iago in Act 1, scene 2. If I did not love Desdemona so much, he says, "I would not my unhoused free condition put into circumscription and confine." The words are revealing. The marriage bond for this warrior is potentially a confinement, not so much enriching his identity, as somehow potentially undercutting it, circumscribing it, and restricting his absolute freedom and autonomy. Only his passionate love for this woman has provoked him to risk marriage.

Let's also remember the rather asymmetrical formula he offers as he explains the way their mutual love began: "She loved me for the dangers I had passed, and I loved her that she did pity them." I loved her because she showed such feeling for my sufferings. She loved me for my endurance and heroism; I loved her for her sympathy. It's as if he doesn't love Desdemona so much as he loves Desdemona's love for him, and as if, perhaps, his sense of self is going to be dependent on his sense that Desdemona does indeed love him. He needs her to mirror him in a certain kind of way; perhaps there's a hint of narcissism here.

Then, let's consider what happens when Othello is ordered off to deal with the Turks and Desdemona makes it clear that staying alone in Venice is not her idea of a honeymoon. She's more outspoken here than with her father. She married the moor to follow him, she says. She has consecrated her soul and fortunes to him, she says. If she's left behind while he goes to the war, she says, "the rites for which I love him are bereft me." Rites, as in marriage ritual, but also, punningly, rights, as in the rights of a wife. She doesn't want to be a wife in name only. She's frank about her desire. She wants sexual consummation, full union with her beloved.

Let's look at what Othello has to say on this topic. He is oddly defensive as he asks that her request be granted. He explicitly claims that his own physical desire is not at issue. He doesn't beg for Desdemona to accompany him, he says, "to please the palate of my appetite." He wishes, instead, to be "free and bounteous to her mind." He also goes out of his way to insist that having his wife along on his mission won't detract from his warrior identity. The day, he says, that the light-winged toys of love corrupt his warrior abilities, the day that lovers' trivia gets in the way of his generalship, then he says, "let housewives use my helmet as a skillet," which suggests that he anticipates some suspicion in the minds of his listeners that his love for his wife may render him effeminate, unable to do his duty, fit only for domestic tasks. He is speaking, in fact, to a kind of anxiety we quite often see in Renaissance writings on love. The masculine fear that simply to love a woman, to care for her too much, might weaken one's manly powers.

There's a little war going on within Othello, as if his notion of himself as warrior leader and his notion of himself as the man who loves and desires Desdemona are somehow at odds. And, if he is divided within, if his sense of self has been fractured by the experience of love, then he is going to be vulnerable to manipulation. Such self-division is exactly the kind of thing that Iago will be able to manipulate and exploit.

To summarize, we seem to see, in Othello, a fear that marriage will be imprisoning, confining, a kind of trap, and a sort of disempowerment. He seems to exhibit a hint of uneasiness at Desdemona's frank articulation of her desire. And then, there's also this whole matter of his loving her because she loves him, which would suggest his love might be dependent on his absolute confidence in her emotional investment in him.

When Brabanzio gave his parting shot about Desdemona, "Look to her, moor, if you have eyes to see, she has deceived her father and may thee," Othello's reply was, "My life upon her faith." It's a pretty extreme declaration of his investment in her fidelity. He stakes his very being on her devotion. And he'll echo this extremity of feeling later in the play, when he says, "Perdition catch my soul but I do love thee and when I love thee not chaos is come again." He offers a near apocalyptic vision of what it would mean to have his love for Desdemona shattered. Watch out to see what use Iago will make of all this.

Lecture Eight
Othello II—Monstrous Births

Scope:

This lecture considers the character of Iago, his plots against Othello, and the longstanding mystery of his "motiveless malignity." It explores Iago's capacity to manipulate other characters' actions through his skillful use of loaded language and his exploitation of the unexamined assumptions and biases instilled in them by their society and culture (their irrational but strongly held prejudices of all kinds). The lecture offers a close analysis of the scenes in which Iago begins to poison Othello's imagination; as Iago leads his commanding officer to suspect both Desdemona and the hapless Cassio, it pays particular attention to the ways in which he plays midwife to the "monstrous birth" of Othello's jealousy.

Outline

I. The workings of Iago's mind are disclosed to us from the very start of *Othello*.

   A. We learn of his hatred toward Othello.

      1. The reasons for this are particularly impenetrable: his revenge goes beyond anything that might be justified by his jealousy over Cassio's promotion.

      2. Iago, in fact, adduces an excess of reasons for his "motiveless malignity" and doesn't seem to care whether they are provable.

   B. We see his ability to mask his private desires and his horrible aims under a façade of honesty and bluntness.

   C. We see his ability to corrupt, transform, and debase anything and anybody through his cunning use of language.

II. Iago is skilled in manipulating and poisoning the minds of others.

   A. He exploits the prejudices and unexamined assumptions already held by others (as with Brabantio).

   B. He makes people see other people as if they are types, not individuals—speaking to Roderigo, he reduces Othello to a "barbarian" and Desdemona to a Venetian woman of sophisticated and debased tastes.

C. He insists on his own cool rationalism while offering irrational arguments that sway others.

D. He is a superb improviser (a quality exemplified by his impromptu plotting during his soliloquies).

E. He exhibits a fearful creativity in "birthing" his monstrous plans.

III. Iago most obviously brings about a terrible transformation of Othello.

A. He changes him from a noble lover to an insanely jealous man and from an imposing warrior to a crazed would-be murderer.

B. He makes Othello think himself a monster: a betrayed husband wearing the horns of the cuckold.

C. Iago's corruption of Othello impregnates his imagination, bringing forth the "green-eyed monster" of jealousy.

IV. In Act 3, Iago deploys a variety of tactics in the long, drawn-out manipulation of his commander that results in Othello's doubting Desdemona's faith.

A. He works by silence and omission as much as direct statement.

B. Iago's suggestive withholding of information permits Othello's own imagination to run riot; he will introduce new topics at random and encourage Othello to piece together a story.

C. He produces subtly revised accounts of actual events (as when he presents Desdemona as the beguiling deceiver of Brabantio, although Brabantio had actually accused *Othello* of using witchcraft against Desdemona).

D. Most horribly, he transforms Desdemona's willingness to love a man across cultural boundaries into evidence of her predisposition to "unnatural" behavior (namely, adultery).

E. He nudges Othello into thinking that his own blackness may now disgust his wife.

V. Having imparted his poison to Othello, Iago is now in a position to make him see only what Iago wants him to see.

Essential Reading:

Shakespeare, *Othello.*

Supplementary Reading:

Introduction to Neill's Oxford edition of *Othello*, pp. 147–169.

Questions to Consider:

1. Iago's horrible ingenuity is made manifest well before he starts to poison Othello's imagination against Desdemona. Discuss the report he gives to Othello of what supposedly happened in the "drinking scene" and his behavior when he offers comfort to the disgraced Cassio.

2. In 3.3., Othello has his first soliloquy of the play ("This fellow's of exceeding honesty..."). Examine the progression of his thoughts and reflections. How logical are the conclusions he reaches?

Lecture Eight—Transcript
Othello II—Monstrous Births

In *Hamlet*, we were invited into the hero's inner life almost from the start. It wasn't until quite late in the play that we got some insight into the workings of Claudius's mind when he contemplated his own evil doings. We were invited, as it were, to become identified with the *Hamlet* perspective. In *Othello*, by contrast, it is the operations of the villain's mind that are revealed to us from the beginning. We have no soliloquy from Othello until Act 3, but Iago soliloquizes at the end of Act 1, scene 3, Act 2, scene 1, and towards the end of Act 2, scene 3.

Three things are made very clear to us about Iago from the beginning: his enmity to Othello; his ability to mask his private desires and his real nature and intentions, under a facade of honesty and bluntness; and his ability to corrupt, to taint, to horribly transform and debase anything and anybody simply through his use of language. This lecture will explore, in some detail, all of these aspects of Iago.

The reason for Iago's hatred for Othello turns out to be peculiarly impenetrable. As the play opens, Iago tells foolish Roderigo, Othello's rival for Desdemona, that Othello has blighted his career prospects. Iago is Othello's ensign, his standard-bearer, senior non-commissioned officer—in our terms, I guess, a kind of career sergeant major. He had hopes of being promoted to the rank of lieutenant, but he's been passed over in favor of Michael Cassio, an inexperienced young nobleman. According to Iago, Cassio is "a great arithmetician," all theory, no practical experience—straight out of ROTC, as it were.

Of course, in a sense, this explanation explains nothing. The destruction Iago goes on to wreak on Othello, Desdemona, and Cassio is out of all proportion to this rationalized grievance. Furthermore, Iago keeps on producing new reasons for hating Othello, which only muddy the waters. For example, in the soliloquy at the end of Act 1, scene 3, he says he suspects Othello of having slept with his own wife, Emilia. In the soliloquy at the end of Act 2, scene 1, he says he desires Desdemona and wishes to even things out with Othello, wife for wife. In the same soliloquy, he says he suspects Cassio has cheated with Emilia, as well. He simply offers too many reasons and none of the sexual ones are substantiated in any way by the text or action. Emilia, in fact, is so concerned to please Iago that she gives him Desdemona's lost handkerchief—which will be fatally important in the plot of the tragedy—even against her better instincts. In fact, Iago eventually says he doesn't really know if Othello has cuckolded him. "I hate the moor and it is thought abroad that twixt my sheets he has done my office. I know not if it be true, but I for mere suspicion in that kind will do as if for surety."

All we can be sure is that Iago hates Othello and wishes to destroy him and all around him. It's as if he is the very incarnation of malice and destructive energy. The poet Coleridge memorably described Iago's "motiveless malignity." There is one point in the play, though, that kind of points me to what's going on with Iago. He says of Cassio, "He hath a daily beauty in his life that makes me ugly." Something about Cassio's easy enjoyment of life makes Iago loathe himself all the more and compels him to destroy him. You can probably extend that to all the people who are seemingly happy in this play.

Iago makes it clear to Roderigo that his whole life is one big play act. When Roderigo doubts that Iago really hates Othello, since he seems to attend upon Othello so faithfully, Iago declares, "In following him I follow but myself. Heaven is my judge, not I for love and duty but seeming so for my peculiar end." He goes on to suggest that when his outward actions actually show what is in his heart, "'tis not long after but I will wear my heart upon my sleeve for daws to pick at." The day you see my appearance match my reality, I'll wear my heart on my sleeve to be picked at by crows and jackdaws.

Note that Roderigo never stops to ask whether Iago is showing a false face to him, as well. Roderigo is what Shakespeare's contemporaries would call a gull and what we would call a sucker. Othello, meanwhile, has no suspicion of Iago's doubleness. He describes him to the duke of Venice as a man of honesty and trust, and both Othello and Cassio are always labeling him good Iago and honest Iago. We hold the discrepancy of awareness. We bear the weight of knowledge as we watch Iago carrying out his poisonous activities. I don't use that word lightly. After all, one of the first tasks Iago sets himself and Rodrigo is to go to Brabanzio, and as Iago puts it, poison his delight. But, unlike the murderous Claudius, Iago doesn't pour something entirely new and horrible into people's ears. He exploits what is already in their minds. The unexamined assumptions and biases instilled in them by their society and culture—their irrational, but strongly held prejudices. As we've already seen him do when he shouted up to Brabanzio that his daughter was copulating with an old black ram, that the devil had taken her.

Iago presents himself as a supreme rationalist or pragmatist. After Othello and Desdemona's marriage has been validated by the duke and Roderigo is whimpering that he is so overwhelmed by his frustrated love for Desdemona that he's about to drown himself, Iago lectures Roderigo on the power of self-control, on will and reason, on not being ruled by one's emotions. "We have reason to cool our raging motions, our carnal stings, our unbitted lusts, whereof I think this that you call love to be a sect or scion."

His attitude towards the very notion of love is telling. For him, it always gets translated into lust, sensual appetite. He informs Roderigo that what Roderigo calls love is just a funny little offshoot of lust. His emphasis on reason has its own irony, though, given the irrationality of his own desire to utterly destroy Othello. But, of course, Iago, the self-proclaimed rationalist, always plays on the irrational in his victims. He does so by making them see their universe in terms of unexamined generalizations, or by looking at people as types, not individuals. Let's look at him working hard to persuade Roderigo that Othello and Desdemona's relationship must be doomed. He wants to do this, of course, so that Roderigo will continue to stick around and will keep funding Iago's plots:

> "Drown thyself? Drown cats and blind puppies. It cannot be long that Desdemona should continue her love to the moor, put money in thy purse. It was a violent commencement in her and thou shalt see an answerable sequestration, put money in thy purse. These moors are changeable in their wills, fill thy purse with money. She must change for youth. When she is sated with his body, she will find the error of her choice. If a frail vow between an erring barbarian and a super subtle Venetian be not too hard for my wits and all the tribe of hell, thou shalt enjoy her, therefore make money."

The slippery argument's full of unproven claims. There's the unexamined assumption that it is only lustful appetite that has drawn Othello and Desdemona together in the first place, and that once that appetite is sated, they'll turn from one another, that because Desdemona is younger than Othello, she must turn to a younger man eventually, that the vows between them are necessarily frail. Iago glides over the fact that Roderigo has presumably just heard Othello say to Brabanzio, "My life upon her faith." Iago insists that Othello is a typical barbarian who has erred, made a mistake, in choosing this fine Venetian lady, and who will err, wander away from her eventually. He also insists that Desdemona herself is a typical Venetian woman whose sophisticated and debased tastes will require new sources of pleasure. You might compare Iago here to Iago in his joking conversation with Desdemona while they await the arrival of Othello's ship in Cyprus, in which Iago reduces all women to the same thing—horny, grasping, and deceptive. And of course, even as Iago offers his slippery comfort, he threads through his arguments with his own interest in Roderigo's finances. As he persuades him to come to Cyprus with him to win Desdemona, put money in thy purse, sucker.

Iago has another skill; he's an improviser. We see him making up his plots as he goes along, bringing them into being before our eyes. Listen to him musing in his soliloquy at the very end of the first act, pondering how to ruin Cassio. "To get his place, how? How? Let's see. After some time to abuse Othello's ears that he is too familiar with his wife. He hath a person and a smooth dispose to be suspected, framed to make women false. The moor is of a free and open nature that thinks men honest that but seem to be so, and will as tenderly be led by the nose as asses are. I have it. It is engendered. Hell and night must bring this monstrous birth to the world's light."

There is a monstrous kind of creativity here as Iago ponders his new idea of fabricating, out of nothing, an adulterous affair between Cassio and Desdemona. The imagery of Iago's concluding lines makes him midwife to a horrible birth. Something will get born out of blackness and not the blackness of pigmented skin, but the moral blackness that belongs to Iago. Look out for other images of birth and monstrosity in this play—a play, which after all, will end up with the spectacle of something horrible lying on a bloodied bed.

So, what does Iago bring to birth? Most obviously, he produces a terrible transformation of Othello. In Act 2, we'd seen the noble lover rapturously greeting his bride in Cyprus, calling her, "Oh my fair warrior, my soul's joy." Iago transforms Othello into the insanely jealous man who can say to Desdemona, "Oh thou weed, who art so lovely fair and smells so sweet, that the sense aches at thee. Would thou hadst never been born." He changes the hero from the imposing warrior who could stop a 17th-century lynch mob with a few words to a man who, by Act 4, is insanely babbling of noses, lips, and handkerchiefs, and overwhelmed by his passions, falling into a kind of fit. He turns Othello into a crazed, would-be murderer who can say of Desdemona, "I will chop her into messes."

Iago makes Othello think of himself as something monstrous, for he makes him believe himself to be a cuckold, a deceived husband. There is a longstanding folk tradition of the cuckold, the guy whose wife is cheating on him and who grows horns that are invisible to himself, but visible to the rest of the world. A horned man's a monster and a beast, says Othello, at one point contemplating his apparent identity as husband of a cheating wife. But, the monster is all of Iago's making. Indeed, the very language of the play suggests this.

Early on in the long drawn out process of poisoning Othello's mind, Iago appears to be holding back key information from the general. "What dost thou think?" says Othello. "Think, my lord?" Iago replies. Othello explodes, "'Think, my lord.' By heaven, thou echoest me, as if there were some monster in thy thought too hideous to be shown." There's a terrible irony here because of course it is the Iago-engendered monster that hides in Iago's mind, the false story of Desdemona and Cassio's affair.

Let's push this a little further. Othello and Iago glimpse Cassio parting from Desdemona. We know that Cassio was innocently visiting her to beg her aid in winning Othello's favor after the disgrace that Iago had brought him into. But, Othello focuses upon Iago's theatrical response to the Desdemona/Cassio connection, remarking, "Thou didst contract and purse thy brow together as though thou then hadst shut up in thy brain some horrible conceit."

Conceit, the word in the 17th century means concept, idea, or thought. It's a word allied with mental processes and other kinds of conception. Iago has conceived his plot, conceived a monster. Now, by making Othello insist on learning his "conceit," he is going to make Othello conceive ill of Desdemona, almost by a process of impregnation.

While we're on the subject of conceiving monsters, another monster that Iago helps to engender is jealousy. He himself says, "Oh beware my lord of jealousy, it is the green eyed monster which doth mock the meat it feeds on." Jealousy, of course, will now possess and feed upon Othello's soul. Emilia, speaking to Desdemona in the next scene, claims that jealousy is a monster begot upon itself, born on itself, self-propagating. But, in truth, it is her own husband who has begotten this jealousy on Othello.

How does Iago achieve this ghastly work of miscreation? First of all, paradoxically, by silence and omission. Or rather, by just saying enough that Othello fills in the gaps in his speech, colors in the picture. At first, Iago never directly says, "I believe Cassio has been sleeping with your wife." It's a long time before he even says "Keep an eye on your wife and Cassio."

The morning after Cassio has been made drunk by Iago, has been drawn into a brawl by Iago's machinations, and has been dismissed from his lieutenancy by Othello, he goes on Iago's suggestion, to beg Desdemona's help in recovering Othello's favor. In Act 3, scene 3, after Desdemona has pretty much persuaded Othello to reinstate Cassio, Iago asks an apparently innocent question: "Did Michael Cassio, when you wooed my lady, know of your love?" Othello says, "He did, from first to last, why dost thou ask?" "But for a satisfaction of my thought, no further harm." "Why of thy thought, Iago?" asks Othello. "I did not think he had been acquainted with her." "Oh yes, and went between us very oft." "Indeed," says Iago.

Iago begins a process of withholding that becomes more and more significant, making Othello beg, demand that he reveal his thoughts. When Othello asks what he thinks of Michael Cassio, Iago replies, "I dare be sworn I think that he is honest." I think so too, says Othello. "Men should be what they seem," says Iago. "Certain, men should be what they seem," says Othello. "Why then I think Cassio's an honest man." I dare be sworn I think that he is honest. Men should be what they seem. Why then I think Cassio's an honest man. Iago's implication, well since he seems honest, I guess he must be so, but he leaves the question dangling.

Often during the conversation, Iago will appear to move off at random to a different topic entirely, that nevertheless adds to the dark story he's inviting Othello to piece together. He'll suddenly, for example, start talking about the absolute importance of good name in man or woman, the sanctity of good reputation. His official meaning is that he must not wantonly blacken anybody's reputation. But, it is as if he is making Othello wonder with his very protestations, what man's name is in danger of being darkened or what woman's.

Another example of this comes when he suddenly says, "Beware, my lord, of jealousy." Jealousy just sorts of floats in there, this abstract noun in isolation and dangles to suggest that Othello has something to be jealous of. Othello is invited to take Iago's word, which has not yet been attached to a person. Your jealousy, my jealousy, and build it into a narrative.

And finally, Iago says, "Look to your wife. Observe her well with Cassio. Wear your eyes thus, not jealous, nor secure. I would not have your free and noble nature out of self bounty be abused. Look to it." "Look to your wife. Observe her well with Cassio." He still forces Othello to fill in the words, observe her well because…

We're presented with the slow, but inexorable poisoning of Othello's imagination. Incidentally, the very leisureliness of this action is one reason that *Othello* is a very difficult play to film. If a movie director makes cuts in the text and compresses this insidious process whereby Iago moves Othello to doubt his wife, he risks making the hero look like an ignoble fool. Shakespeare gives Iago a lot of space in which to work his horrible magic.

Iago, having raised preliminary doubts in Othello's mind about his wife and Cassio, then adds to this a different strategy. A strategy already familiar to us from his conversations with Roderigo, that of erasing the individual, ignoring Desdemona's unique qualities and her manifest goodness and working instead with stereotypes and unexamined assumptions about human nature or Venetian women. His speech continues: "In Venice they do let God see the pranks they dare not show their husbands. Their best conscience is not to leave it undone but keep it unknown." In Venice, "they," women—we all know what Venetian women are like. He's drawing on the city's general reputation for certain kind of sexual promiscuity that was mainly associated with the courtesans, the high-class prostitutes.

Then he begins to turn the screw. She did deceive her father marrying you and when she seemed to shake and fear your looks, she loved them most. He reprises Brabanzio's words of Act 1, scene 3, but he also erases Othello's own passionate assertion, "She had eyes and chose me." A positive act of loving choice is reconstructed or refocused as a transgressive act of deception and Iago also cleverly takes up another aspect of Brabanzio's accusations. "She that so young could give out such a seeming to seal her father's eyes up, he thought it witchcraft." Iago is suggesting that Brabanzio thought it was witchcraft that he couldn't tell Desdemona was in love with Othello, but Othello seems to forget here that it was he, Othello, who was accused of using a kind of black magic by Brabanzio to seduce the lady. Brabanzio never accused his daughter of using evil charms to deceive him. Desdemona's heroic love that crosses boundaries, takes risks, is gradually and paradoxically transformed by Iago into evidence of her willingness to transgress, to deceive. And Othello has now been nudged towards the position Brabanzio took in Act 1.

We can push this further. Remember Brabanzio's constant recurrence in Act 1 to the notion of Desdemona's "unnatural" behavior, his refusal to believe that there was anything natural in Desdemona's falling in love with Othello? Iago also exploits this, as well. "I do not think but Desdemona's honest," says Othello. I cannot but think that Desdemona is honest. And the word honest, incidentally, has a broader connotation than in modern English when applied to a woman. A woman's honesty is not only her lack of deceitfulness, but her chastity, whether that means her virginity, or, as in this case, the virtuous monogamy of a married woman.

But Othello goes on: "And yet how nature erring from itself." He's musing as if speaking in general about the way we may act against our better nature. Iago then intervenes, kidnaps his terms and refocuses the whole business of unnatural behavior in terms of Desdemona's marriage to Othello. "Ay, there's the point; as to be bold with you, not to affect many proposed matches of her own clime, complexion, and degree, whereto we see in all things nature tends. Foh! One may smell in such a will most rank, foul disproportion, thoughts unnatural."

Iago's argument is that one can see, in Desdemona's refusal to marry anybody of her own ethnicity, and nationality, and social rank, a willful perversity and unnatural desires. That there is something inherently very wrong about the very fact she chose Othello. And as this speech continues, he will also ask, may she not come to repent that she has swerved from the natural behavior of a noble Venetian lady?

This, for me, is one of the most terrible moments in this play. Othello is invited to accept that the very fact that she had loved a black man means that she, by definition, has a perverse, erring disposition and that she may naturally turn back to prefer more natural objects of desire than Othello. The result of it is that only about 30 lines later Othello is saying, perhaps it is because I am black that she has stopped loving me, but he's always been black and he himself has said, she had eyes and chose him.

"She had eyes and chose me." Othello loses sight of Desdemona's loving vision. Instead, his own inner eye becomes filled with the horrible visions Iago offers to him until he can only see Desdemona as the promiscuous liar Iago has created out of nothing. I'll have more to say about just what Iago does to Othello's eyes in my next lecture.

Lecture Nine
Othello III—"Ocular Proof"

Scope:

What aspects of Othello's own psyche and of the universe he inhabits lead him to choose an unholy alliance with Iago over a resolute belief in his wife's fidelity? This lecture looks more closely at the gender dynamics of this play, establishing some cultural contexts for thinking about the anxieties and suspicions that Iago exploits in Othello and for the link that Othello himself articulates between Desdemona's ostensible betrayal of their love and the destruction of his warrior identity. It will also develop at greater length a topic touched on in the previous lecture, analyzing Shakespeare's finely nuanced representation of Othello's poisoned sight and corrupted imagination and examining in particular the "handkerchief plot" as it develops in Acts 3 and 4.

Outline

I. Tragedy often focuses upon highly fraught moments of choice.

   A. Othello declares that he is torn between believing in Desdemona's honesty (which means her chastity, as well as her faith) and believing in Iago's integrity and good judgment.

   B. He insists on having proof—but that proof will be mediated by Iago.

II. In addition to Iago's manipulative actions, other forces in the world of this play help to make Othello choose as he does.

   A. The workings of chance help Iago—for example, Desdemona's accidental loss of her handkerchief.

   B. Human fallibility helps Iago—for example, Emilia's desire to gain a kind word from him by giving him the lost handkerchief.

   C. People's own virtues may undo them—Iago uses Desdemona's generous sympathy for Cassio against her.

   D. The fertility of other people's imaginations aids Iago—their ability to make their own monsters.

III. But Iago also makes use of Othello's demand for "ocular proof" that Desdemona is untrue.

    A. Without actually offering any material evidence, Iago makes Othello "see" what he fears by spinning a story of Cassio talking in his sleep about a tryst with Desdemona.

    B. The "ocular proof" that Othello is eventually given is an interchange between Cassio and Iago that Othello does not fully hear.

    C. Iago's fabrication of this proof is helped by the fortuitous appearance of Cassio's mistress, Bianca, brandishing Desdemona's handkerchief.

    D. Othello sees nothing of Desdemona's supposed infidelity, only the lost handkerchief. The object becomes equated with her lost honor and with Cassio's supposed possession of her.

IV. Othello's choice to believe that Iago is honest and Desdemona false has immediate consequences.

    A. He invokes the infernal powers of vengeance and enters into a terrible covenant of revenge with Iago.

    B. He transforms Desdemona into a "fair devil" whose white skin masks blackness within.

    C. He asserts that the purity of his own name has been begrimed by Desdemona's actions.

V. Othello's insistence that Desdemona's actions have transformed him into something infamous seems to be related to some anxieties that are located not so much in race as in gender.

    A. He cries out against husbands' inability to possess and control the desires of their wives (even though his society officially makes husbands the "owners" of their wives' bodies).

    B. It is crucially important for Othello to believe that Desdemona is true: he has declared that "chaos will come again" when he ceases to love her.

    C. He cannot bear to be identified by other men as a man who has failed to possess his wife exclusively.

    D. He now believes his warrior "occupation" to have been undone by her infidelity.

E. He also believes that the only way to end her power to hurt him—and to reestablish control over her—is to kill her.

VI. The play offers an alternative model of how one might respond to jealous suspicions.

    A. When Bianca suspects Cassio of involvement with another woman, she confronts him directly.

    B. She does not attempt to discover the identity of her putative rival or to seek revenge.

VII. It is sometimes argued that Othello's choice is determined by his soldier identity.

    A. He is inexperienced in matters of the heart.

    B. He automatically trusts the comrade whom he has known for a long time.

    C. Nevertheless, he makes an important strategic decision based on flimsy evidence.

VIII. It has also been suggested that the central opposition in the play is not, in fact, Iago versus Othello but men versus women.

    A. In a world where men seek to control women's bodies and their speech, Othello's eventual suffocation of Desdemona silences the tongue with which she protests her innocence.

    B. Desdemona's apparently problematic passivity—her silence in the face of Othello's abuse until her last hour—is, ironically, exactly the kind of behavior required of virtuous wives in Shakespeare's society.

    C. Desdemona's generous response to Emilia's suspicions that someone has slandered her to Othello suggests a striking discrepancy between male and female perspectives in this play.

    D. Shakespeare scholar Carol Neely suggests that in *Othello*, female attitudes toward men tend to be overindulgent, while male attitudes toward women are brutally suspicious.

    E. In the gap between these perspectives, the tragedy moves toward its climax.

Essential Reading:

Shakespeare, *Othello*.

Supplementary Reading:

Neely, *Broken Nuptials in Shakespeare's Plays*, chapter 3.

Questions to Consider:

1. Trace the movements of Desdemona's lost handkerchief through the action of the play. What kind of significance does it accrue, and what do you make of the story Othello tells about its origin?

2. After Othello abuses Desdemona as if she were a common prostitute in 4.2., Shakespeare gives us an exchange among Desdemona, Emilia, and Iago. Discuss the distinctive ways in which Emilia and Iago react to Desdemona's plight.

Lecture Nine—Transcript
Othello III—"Ocular Proof"

Choosing is always a very loaded business in tragedy. Tragic dramas may focus the matter differently. They may imagine a universe where there are perhaps no right choices, as in *Hamlet*. They may explore in great detail the unfolding consequences of a swift or rash decision. Or, they may dissect out, in agonizing detail, the making of a choice. This is what we are offered in *Othello* and Othello himself articulates his moral dilemma in Act 3, scene 3. "I think my wife be honest, and think she is not. I think that thou art just, and think thou art not. I'll have some proof." I'll reemphasize once more that double meaning of honest, both without deceit and also sexually faithful. Who should he believe? Desdemona or Iago? I'll have some proof, he says.

I'm going to talk about the business of proof in this lecture, but I want to begin by looking at some of the forces that even Iago can't completely control—not only matters of happenstance or coincidence, the kind of cosmic bad luck one often sees in tragedy, but also the prevailing conditions that in the world Shakespeare creates may make Othello choose as he does. I'll eventually be exploring in larger detail and setting in historical context these forces that also contribute to Othello's predicament.

Let's start by thinking about some of the small chance happenings that end up making their own contribution towards the evil Iago has unleashed in this universe. There's the matter of Desdemona's handkerchief, Othello's gift, which goes missing. And I think I should say a word about Renaissance handkerchiefs at this point, which were rather a bigger deal than our handkerchiefs, pieces of very beautiful, expensive linen, often elaborately embroidered and usually only carried by the upper classes.

After Iago has started to poison his mind, Othello has an encounter with Desdemona in which—and there's a bitter irony here if you think of that whole business of the cuckold's horns—he disguises his distracted behavior by telling her he has a headache. Desdemona takes her handkerchief to make a kind of pressure bandage for Othello's forehead, but when he pushes her away, she lets it drop. So, she loses it in the very process of showing her loving concern for her husband. But, Iago will turn its loss into evidence that she is untrue, by making sure that Othello sees the handkerchief in Cassio's hands. Iago's aided, of course, by the human fallibility of Emilia who picks it up and then gives it to Iago just to get a kind word from him, but who fails to find out what exactly he wants it for.

This unfortunate combination of Desdemona's own loving kindness and mere mischance may remind us of the way that people's own virtues can undo them in the universe of tragedy. At the end of the scene in which he has advised Cassio to ask Desdemona's aid in regaining the favor of Othello, Iago gloats, I will turn her virtue into pitch and out of her own goodness make the net that shall enmesh them all. Pitch is black tar. He will exploit her generosity of spirit for his own purposes, make white look black by arguing that she pleads for Cassio's reinstatement because she desires him. And of course, he benefits from the fact that when Othello eventually presses Desdemona threateningly about the absence of the handkerchief, she nervously tries to change the subject by redoubling her pleas on Cassio's behalf. Every time Othello says, "the handkerchief," she tries to make her husband promise to reinstate Cassio as his lieutenant. And every time she mentions Cassio's name, she unwittingly reminds Othello of Iago's lie that he had seen the handkerchief in Cassio's possession.

We might also recognize the sheer fertility of the human imagination, the way it can create its own monsters and turn them into reality. Relatively early in Iago's beguiling of him, Othello says, "I'll see before I doubt." Two hundred and fifty lines later, he says, "Now do I see 'tis true." But what does he see? Iago does encourage people to see things, but he makes them conjure them up in their imaginations rather than in any absolute material reality. We've already seen his tactics with Brabanzio, the creation of a nightmare fantasy of his daughter in the arms of a bestial alien.

Othello does not succumb immediately and lock stock and barrel to Iago's manipulation. He resists to a certain extent; he even threatens Iago with death if he is slandering Desdemona without proper cause. "Give me ocular proof!" he commands. Make me see the truth of what you are insinuating. Iago adopts an air of helpful puzzlement: "Would you...behold her topp'd?" I don't think I can quite manage that. The verb *topped* is a variant on tupped and would usually refer to animals copulating. As usual, Iago makes everything as suggestively degraded as possible. Even though Cassio's supposed affair with Desdemona is totally unproven, the very words of Iago's question will encourage Othello to have horrible thoughts of Desdemona with another man, something that Iago builds upon when he tells Othello a completely fabricated story.

He and Cassio have apparently shared the same quarters, and I should mention at this point that, in an age when beds were rather scarcer items of furniture than they are nowadays, it was much more common for people who were unrelated to one another to share them. Iago tells Othello:

> "I lay with Cassio lately and being troubled with a raging tooth, I could not sleep. There are a kind of men so loose of soul that in their sleeps will mutter their affairs. One of this kind is Cassio. In sleep I heard him say, 'Sweet Desdemona, let us be wary, let us hide our loves.' And then, sir, would he grip and wring my hand, cry 'Oh sweet creature,' and then kiss me hard, lay his leg over my thigh, and sigh and kiss and then cry, 'Cursed fate that gave thee to the moor.'"

His word painting agonizes Othello and Iago remarks that this may help to add substance to other proofs, but there are no proofs. There's only this astonishingly evocative alternative reality created by Iago's language. We don't know that Iago ever shared a bed with Cassio. The picture he paints is so horribly effective that Othello doesn't even pause to contemplate the nonsense of Cassio's supposed cry, "Oh cursed fate that gave thee to the moor." It makes it sound as if Desdemona has been married off against her will, quite contradicting Iago's earlier discussion of the supposed willfulness of Desdemona's choice of Othello. And finally, Iago claims to have seen Cassio carrying Desdemona's prized handkerchief, the love token embroidered with little strawberries that she received from Othello, the token Iago himself has taken care should come into Cassio's possession.

Othello only has hearsay evidence at this point and we get more hearsay evidence in Act 4, where Othello asks Iago if Cassio has spoken of Desdemona. "'Hath he said anything?' 'He hath, my lord. But be you well assured, no more than he'll unswear.' 'What hath he said?' 'Faith, that he did. I know not what he did?' 'What, what? Lie, with her?' 'With her, on her, what you will.'" And Othello's own imagination does the rest.

What ocular proof does Othello have in the end? He showed an interchange between Cassio and Iago, which he does not hear. If you remember, Iago has positioned Othello supposedly to see Iago engage Cassio in a conversation about Desdemona. What actually happens is that Iago and Cassio get into some heavy-duty locker room chat about Cassio's mistress, the besotted Bianca, while Othello watches at a distance believing they're talking about Desdemona. He can see them. He can hear their rather lewd laughter. He can't hear the exact words they're saying. And this, of course, is always quite a problematic thing in the staging of the play. The director has got to make it convincing that Othello is sort of getting a sight and a general impression, but not hearing all the words. Maybe the odd word would come to him.

Now, we hear what Othello thinks is happening because we have the benefit of his agonized remarks aside, "Now he tells how she plucked him to my chamber." But, at the same time, stage convention allows us to hear what is really being said by Iago and Cassio. And once again, pure chance helps Iago when Bianca storms in to interrupt the conversation in front of Othello's very eyes, brandishing the handkerchief whose embroidered design Cassio has asked her to copy, so that Iago can then can rub salt in Othello's wounds by suggesting that not only has Cassio messed around with Desdemona, but that he also values her so little, he's given her supposed gift to his other woman. Othello sees nothing of Desdemona's supposed infidelity. He sees only a sign for it, the handkerchief. The handkerchief, as it moves from hand to hand, becomes equated with Desdemona's virtue, her honor, her body, her love, and Othello is invited to think Cassio now possesses those, just as he possesses the token of Othello's affection, the handkerchief.

Let's return to Othello's agonized articulation of his dilemma. "I think my wife be honest, and I think she is not. I think that thou are art just and think thou art not. I'll have some proof." He has his moment of choice. He chooses to accept secondhand knowledge and hearsay as proof, to believe Iago and to give his allegiance to Iago. And when he does so, it is as if he enters into a kind of terrible, alternative marriage with Iago.

At the very end of Act 3, scene 3, Othello invokes the powers of darkness. In another of the play's deep ironies, he's turned into the thing that he had proved to Brabanzio he wasn't: "Arise, black vengeance from the hollow hell," he cries, swearing he will not rest until he has achieved his revenge and Iago asks the heavens to bear witness that he will follow any order of Othello's to aid him in this. "I am your own for ever," Iago declares, offering a terrible parody of the marriage sacrament as the two men exchange vows.

Othello swears to murder Desdemona, whom he now calls the fair devil and, so doing, re-invokes the language of black and white. Desdemona has become a kind of whited sepulcher, a marble edifice with rottenness and decay within, a woman whose pale, pale skin conceals a heart of darkness. This fair devil, though, is just another monster of Iago's creation, when in reality, Iago is the fair devil, his ostensibly honest outside covering his black lies.

The very particular effect of Desdemona's supposed infidelity on Othello has, in fact, already been articulated by the general in black and white terms. Earlier in the play, faced with Iago's insinuations, he declared, "My name that was as fresh as Dian's visage, is now begrimed and black as my own face."

Dian's visage—the phrase evokes the virgin goddess Diana, patroness of the moon. My good name, says Othello, which was as pure and white as the face of the moon has been rendered filthy. The black/white imagery is very telling here because Othello had wanted to distinguish his identity, his name, and his reputation from his skin color. He seems, in fact, to have internalized the white Venetians' easy assumption about the significance of black outsides. He now considers his good name utterly blackened in a manner that reinforces the cultural connotations of his skin color. But, since it is Desdemona who has supposedly done the dark deeds, why not speak of her blackened name here? Why not say something like "Her name is now as black as my face"? In fact, the printer of a 1630 quarto edition of the play changed the pronoun from the way it appears in the very first printed version of the work to offer this interpretation, as if he thought it would make more sense that way. But, if we stick with that earlier text, with Othello saying "my name," we might want to take Othello at his word and ask, why does Desdemona's action so change his identity, so blacken it, that his only recourse is to destroy her?

It is a teasing, complicated moment. As I've already suggested, it reminds us of Othello's physical blackness. Iago had already manipulated Othello into thinking that the very fact that Desdemona had married a black man suggested there was something perverse and unnatural about her. Now, Othello himself suggests that somehow Desdemona's actions are blackening him in a new way, both tainting his reputation and turning him into an object of abhorrence and mockery—a nightmare version of the shadowy barbarian or naturally debased creature he may fear, at some level, that the white Venetians always think that he is.

Yet, something else that might help to explain what's going on here occurs earlier in Act 3, scene 3, when Othello, in agony, cries out, "Oh curse of marriage, that we can call these delicate creatures ours and not their appetites." The position that Othello finds so cursed is presented as a general situation, but not a universal situation. It is a gendered dilemma; his "we" refers to male human beings only. It invokes the anxieties of a world where men may call these delicate creatures "ours," be the owners of a woman's body, but are also faced with the fact that even if their society gives them authority over their wives, they may still never know the woman's desires, never own her will completely. They cannot control her secret appetites.

Othello is seemingly appalled by a new recognition that men may never be able to control the desires of their women, never be able to keep their bodies loyal to one man, and never be quite sure that the territory of a wife's body is not invaded by others, and for Othello, this is terribly important because he has invested his identity in Desdemona. He had said to Brabanzio, "My life upon her faith." He had said to her, "When I love thee not chaos is come again."

Now, he doubts her faith, and it is not just that he loathes the fact that no man can really be certain that he possesses a woman wholly. It is also that he, Othello, cannot bear being identified by others as a man who has failed to possess Desdemona exclusively. He can't bear the kind of vulnerability that the position of a deceived husband brings. This is the blackening of his name that so horrifies him, his new identity as the husband of a faithless wife, his new identity as a despised cuckold.

In Act 1, scene 3, he had already canvassed the possibility that his love and desire might threaten his warrior virtues. Now, he thinks he has been exposed as one who has given his love to one who has betrayed him and he feels, as a consequence, that he is no longer a warrior. Desdemona's transgression impinges upon his identity. It is as if a threat of female infidelity is also a threat against the masculine sense of self. Othello seems to think he can only be a real man when he is utterly confident of controlling Desdemona's affections. This is why he believes his name to have been darkened. He says, at one point, "I had been happy if the general camp had tasted her sweet body, so I had nothing known. Oh now forever farewell the tranquil mind, farewell content, farewell the plumed troops, and the big wars that makes ambition virtue. Othello's occupation's gone." He had suggested a tension between his identity as a warrior and his identity as a husband. Now that he's a betrayed husband, he's no longer a warrior. Othello's occupation's gone.

The logic which shapes his conclusions here is dependent on the particular nature of the cultural forces that have made him what he is and the very particular way he has gone about constructing his identity and he now feels the only way to end Desdemona's power to hurt him, to cripple his identity, is to kill her. He can only think of reestablishing his control over her body in that most extreme fashion.

The critic Carol Neely, who has written a very fine account of the politics of gender in this play, has noted that there's another person in this play for whom Cassio's coming into possession of Desdemona's handkerchief becomes a cause for jealousy—the Cypriot woman, Bianca. Bianca, whose name, interestingly, is Italian for white, and she's labeled a whore by her society. She's an unmarried woman who supports herself by making her favors available to the Venetian garrison in Cyprus and she is, at present, Cassio's mistress. Cassio gives the strawberry-spotted handkerchief to her after he finds it lying about his lodging and he asks her to copy its design. She suspects it is a gift from another woman, and as I've already noted, ends up throwing it back in Cassio's face. In fact, Bianca goes on the rampage. "What did you mean by that handkerchief that you gave me? I was a fine fool to take it. A likely piece of work that you should find it in your chamber and know not who left it there. This is some minx's token."

Neely points out that when Bianca's jealous, she has it out immediately and explicitly to Cassio's face, something Othello never does with Desdemona until the very moment he's about to kill her. Afterwards, her affections are unchanged. She ends up inviting

Cassio to dine with her that night. Nor does she try to discover the identity of her rival or to get revenge. Bianca is treated as a pretty contemptible object by all the men in the play, including Cassio himself, but she deals with her jealousy much less destructively than they do.

Othello's response to his jealousy is not to confront Desdemona, but to strike up an unholy alliance with Iago, to bond with him and resolve to kill Desdemona. There is a body of argument that defends Othello's action. Some critics have noted that Othello has little experience in matters of the heart. He has lived a life of action in male company and has had no chance to spend much time with women. He automatically trusts the good soldier whom he's probably known much longer than Desdemona. His soldier identity determines a lot of his responses. But, if we accept the logic of these arguments, we might also at least consider the possibility that it would be a very bad general who made an important strategical decision on the flimsy evidence that persuades Othello to destroy his wife. Iago's fine spun case would certainly never have persuaded Hamlet, for example.

As Othello enters into this fiendish bond with Iago, we might also ask just what it is about Othello's psyche and about the world that Othello inhabits that makes the ostensibly obvious or understandable move for him the choice to trust Iago not Desdemona, for Othello's tragedy is as much shaped by his choice to ally himself with Iago as his decision to kill his wife. Neely suggests that the central opposition in this play is not so much Iago versus Othello as men versus women. For one of the things Iago has done is incorporate Othello within a community of men who can deplore the fact that "we can call these delicate creatures ours and not their appetites," men who yearn to possess a woman wholly and yet are terrified of the female agency and female desire, which may endanger that absolute possession. This is a world where men seek to control women's bodies and their speech. Othello exacts the ultimate control over a woman's actions when he suffocates the body he fears has betrayed him and silences the tongue with which Desdemona protests her innocence.

Incidentally, some readers of the play criticize Desdemona's apparent passivity, her patience under Othello's verbal cruelty towards its end, but in terms of the cultural prescriptions of early

©2007 The Teaching Company.

modern Europe, she is doing exactly what a virtuous woman is supposed to—that is, to sustain her husband's cruelty with patience.

There is a particularly horrific sequence in Act 4 when Othello interrogates Emilia as if she was the madam of a brothel and Desdemona one of her stable of women for sale. He goes on to verbally assault Desdemona as if she were indeed the most debased of women. After he has left Desdemona in a state of near collapse, Emilia speculates that some busy and insinuating rogue has devised a slanderous story about her lady, that Desdemona is the victim of some spiteful villain determined to do her wrong. Shakespeare is pressing the irony of the situation to the limit as Emilia gets so, so close to the truth without imagining it could be her own husband who's done this. But, Desdemona simply and swiftly responds, "If any such there be, heaven pardon him."

Her words are astonishingly generous given what she has just suffered at her husband's hands. And it can only make us ponder the scene in which Othello takes his own terrible vow to slay his wife. Heaven pardon her are not words which rise to his lips. It suggests a striking gap—a gap that Neely writes about at some length—between male and female perspectives in this play. Male stories about women, as we have seen, tend to be anxious, distrustful, suspicious. Female attitudes towards men tend to be rather over generous because even the shrewd Emilia doesn't apparently anticipate, when she dutifully delivers over that handkerchief to her husband, that he could want it for some evil purpose.

Men and women in this play can seem at times like two different races, speaking different languages. In the gap that opens up between them, the tragedy moves to its climax and to the awful revelations that await Othello and it is there that I shall be taking us in my next lecture.

Lecture Ten
Othello IV—Tragic Knowledge

Scope:

This lecture focuses on the play's final act, beginning with a close reading of the soliloquy in which Othello contemplates the murder of his sleeping wife and positions himself as both her judge and her executioner. It discusses the relentless process by which Othello's eyes are opened to Iago's deceptions, emphasizing in particular the alternative perspective on Desdemona offered by her loyal waiting-woman, Emilia. The lecture also juxtaposes Iago's refusal to offer an explanation of his actions with Othello's own attempts to make sense of events that conclude in his suicide. What *does* Othello "know" by the end of his tragedy—and should we permit him to have the last word on his own experience?

Outline

I. *Othello* ends more abruptly than any other tragedy of Shakespeare.

    A. After the hero commits suicide, nobody eulogizes him.

    B. Lodovico's remark (looking at Othello and Desdemona's bodies on the bed)—"This object poisons sight"—reminds us that the spectacle of a black man embracing a white woman has been presented as a kind of poison from the very beginning of the play.

    C. This suggests that Iago's poison is still working.

II. In the last scenes of the play, Othello finds it difficult to process any information that contradicts his own transformed (and tainted) vision of the universe.

    A. His language turns Desdemona's body into a text of his own writing in the brothel scene.

    B. He also rewrites his own identity, presenting himself, in the play's last act, not as a murderer but as an agent of heavenly justice carrying out a ritual sacrifice.

    C. In his stately soliloquy, as he prepares to kill the sleeping Desdemona, he insists that he is at once cleansing the world of her and purging her soul.

D. When Othello offers Desdemona the chance to confess her sins and she insists upon her innocence, he silences her by killing her.

E. He is astonished that there is no cosmic response to his fulfillment of heaven's purposes.

III. The revelations of Act 5 rewrite the story of which Othello considered himself to be the avenging hero, and he must make sense of what has happened.

A. He raises the possibility that Iago is a devil—but is left confronting the problem of human evil.

B. Iago refuses to explain his actions, declaring "what you know you know."

C. This leaves us asking: what *does* Othello know at the last?

IV. Othello attempts to process his "tragic knowledge" in a final summation of his experience.

A. His very last words have him reenacting a long-ago stabbing of a Turk: he divides his identity between the valorous servant of the state and the enemy alien as he kills himself.

B. But before he reaches that moment of self-purgation, he gives his own version of his story.

    1. He characterizes himself as one who loved "too well" but begs the question of why his love could not encompass mercy and forgiveness.

    2. He characterizes himself as "one not easily jealous" and implicitly places murderous responsibility upon the man who "wrought" him from his proper state.

V. If we look more closely at Othello's choice to believe Iago rather than Desdemona, it is helpful to contrast his behavior with that of Emilia.

A. Emilia's instinctive and immediate response to being told that Iago has given Othello proof of Desdemona's infidelity is to declare that her husband lied and that Desdemona was true.

B. Emilia refuses to accept Othello's self-definition as agent of divine justice.

VI. Act 5 offers further evidence of male responses to "transgressive" female speech.

    A. When Desdemona briefly revives and selflessly denies that Othello has killed her, Othello declares her a damnable liar.

    B. When Emilia challenges Othello's account of Desdemona's infidelity, he threatens her with violence.

    C. When Emilia speaks out and demonstrates Iago's guilt, he calls her "whore" and kills her.

VII. The selfless speeches with which both Desdemona and Emilia end their lives contrast strikingly with the self-centeredness of Othello's last speech.

    A. Othello claims the right to write his own history, to explain his actions, and to kill himself on his own terms.

    B. Othello's narrative offers a story in which Iago is not named and Desdemona is invoked only by metaphor: it is as if he is the only player in the drama.

VIII. This returns us to the question of Othello's "tragic knowledge" and of what he "knows" at the end of the play.

    A. Having originally personified himself as divine justice, he now insists on the utter blackness of his sin and assumes that after his death, the spirit of Desdemona will hurl his soul to hell.

    B. His vision of Desdemona is once again phrased in black and white terms and ignores her last forgiving words.

    C. Emilia has insisted upon Desdemona's absolute love for him, but Othello does not ever seem to recognize that such love would not refuse forgiveness.

Essential Reading:

Shakespeare, *Othello*.

Supplementary Reading:

Neill, "Unproper Beds: Race, Adultery and the Hideous in *Othello*," in *Shakespeare's Middle Tragedies: A Collection of Critical Essays*, David Young, ed., pp. 117–145.

Questions to Consider:

1. Reread the scene in which Emilia attends on her mistress before Desdemona retires to bed. How does it develop or complicate the mood of the unfolding tragedy?

2. Do *you* find Othello's summing up of his own tragic experience at the end of the play persuasive and accurate?

Lecture Ten—Transcript
Othello IV—Tragic Knowledge

Othello ends more abruptly than any other tragedy of Shakespeare's. After the hero commits suicide, nobody eulogizes him. There's no equivalent to Fortinbras saying that Hamlet would have made a fine king and bidding his soldiers give him a warrior's burial. The Venetian emissary, Lodovico, looking at the spectacle of Othello and Desdemona lying dead on their marriage bed, simply says: "The object poisons sight. Let it be hid" and then starts giving orders for the appropriation of Othello's wealth by Desdemona's uncle Graziano and the torturing of Iago to death.

The object poisons sight. Of course, the vision of the black man embracing the white woman, whether in love or in death, has been presented as a kind of poison from the start of the play—from the moment that Iago fills Brabanzio's mind with a degraded vision of his daughter making love to Othello, a vision that fuels all his prejudices. Lodovico's response to the bloodstained bed with its dead bodies may recall to us Iago's threat to engender a monstrous birth and bring it to the light. Now, the image of Othello and Desdemona in their final embrace—and let us remember that Othello kisses Desdemona as he dies—is to be hidden as quickly as possible from the respectable gaze of Venice. Iago's poison is working to the very last.

Even if we try to forget the extremity and pathology of Lodovico's reaction, this is nevertheless an almost unbearable play. As I said three lectures earlier, I find it the most painful of Shakespeare's tragedies to see staged and, in particular, the last two acts, in which we move inexorably towards Othello's destruction of Desdemona and his subsequent horrific enlightenment.

In the last scenes of the play, there's relatively little talk between Iago and Othello. Once Iago has successfully impregnated his master's mind with various horrors, Othello becomes unable to process any information which contradicts his transformed vision of his universe in general and of his wife in particular. Indeed, his own language, like Iago's, now attempts to transform reality to fit into his worldview. Thus, we have the horrible encounter of Act 4, scene 2, in which he behaves as if his wife is a whore and he is one of her clients. As Desdemona is reduced to tears by his vicious words to

©2007 The Teaching Company.

her, he accuses her of the rankest kind of promiscuity, and as he looks upon her white face, he asks, "Was this fair paper, this most goodly book, made to write whore upon?" He's horrified that her white skin may now be a kind of blank page for men to write upon her a new identity as a prostitute. But, it is he who has turned her body into a kind of text and he is rewriting her to fit into the story he believes is unfolding, the story of her promiscuity and infidelity.

So, Othello is now utterly caught up in this story of his own making in which he will not be Desdemona's murderer, but an agent of heavenly justice. During the scene in which he speaks to her as if she were a woman of easy virtue, he'd cried out, "Heaven truly knows that thou art false as hell." He took it upon himself to speak for heaven, to speak for God himself. You might compare this to Hamlet telling Gertrude that God has designated him his scourge and minister, the one who punishes wrongdoers and who ministers to diseased souls in Denmark. And indeed, when Othello enters Desdemona's bedroom in the play's last scene, he enters in his role as minister of divine justice. He is no longer the crazed figure of Act 4. His language is again as stately and dignified as when we saw him in Act 1. As his wife sleeps, he soliloquizes. "It is the cause. It is the cause, my soul. Let me not name it to you, you chaste stars. It is the cause."

The cause of his actions is Desdemona's purported infidelity and he won't even name it in case he blackens the pure lights of heaven. "Yet, I'll not shed her blood, nor scar that whiter skin of hers than snow and smooth as monumental alabaster. Yet she must die, else she'll betray more men. Put out the light and then put out the light. If I quench thee, thou flaming minister, I can again thy former light restore should I repent me, but once put out thy light, thou cunningest pattern of excelling nature, I know not where is that Promethean heat that can thy light relume. When I have plucked thy rose, I cannot give it vital growth again. It needs must wither. I'll smell thee on the tree." And he kisses her. "Oh, balmy breath that dost almost persuade justice to break her sword. One more, one more." And, he takes another kiss. "Be thus when thou art dead, and I will kill thee and love thee after."

He's about to do a terrible thing and he articulates it in unbearably tender verse. He has reorganized his universe to accommodate the notion of Desdemona as mortal sinner. He is now her judge, confessor, executioner, acting more in sorrow than in anger, punishing her body in order to purge, cleanse, and save her soul. He claims to be cleansing the world. She must die, else she'll betray more men, and he is still half hypnotized by the whiteness of the flesh that he can no longer believe reflects her moral condition. He cannot refrain from kissing her. He has given himself, godlike, the power over life and death. "Put out the light," he says. Iago has made him an uncreator. If he quenches the torch he carries, he can illuminate it again, but once he puts out the light of Desdemona's life, there will be no going back, there will be no reanimating her.

He links himself to a personification of Justice. And his wife's breath smells so sweet, he might almost be swayed to spare her "to break the sword of justice." And he also sees himself as Desdemona's confessor. After she awakes, he keeps asking her to admit her sins, to offer repentance. He insists on the ritual of penitence before execution. I would not kill thy soul, and we might remember, of course, that a condemned criminal is always given access to a priest so that he or she can undergo confession before execution. Only now, as Othello prepares to kill his wife, does he actually speak directly to Desdemona of Cassio and of her supposed gift of that handkerchief to him, and when she denies she has been false, he won't listen. When she cries out that she never loved Cassio except within the proper bounds of friendly decency, he responds, "By heaven, I saw my handkerchief in his hand. Oh perjured woman! Thou dost stone my heart and makes me call what I intend to do a murder, which I thought a sacrifice."

If she doesn't confess her sins, she'll turn his heart to stone and force him to do brutal murder where he thought to do ritual sacrifice and refusing to hear her pleas, he smothers her. Once she is dead, Othello, still believing he is heaven's minister, cannot believe that his action hasn't produced a cosmic reaction. "Methinks it should be now a huge eclipse of sun and moon," he says. The entire universe should be responding to the deed. But, he will learn all too soon that he hasn't been fulfilling the heavens' purposes. He has merely been the pawn of Iago.

When I discussed the ending of *Hamlet*, I noted how important it is for the prince that the true story of his actions lives on after him. He urgently desires that Horatio report him right. I used this to raise the question of whether the complicated experience represented by the play can be circumscribed by one unambiguous narrative articulated by a figure within the play's action. Othello doesn't have a Horatio. He is isolated, groping for truth, as the last act of his tragedy turns the drama, in which he thought he was the avenging hero, topsy-turvy. He is now obliged to make sense of the other plot that Iago has placed him in—the plot in which he's not a servant of heavenly justice, but the dupe of Iago's hellish malevolence.

When Othello has his last confrontation with Iago, he says, "I look down towards his feet, but that's a fable." For Othello, the only possible explanation of what's happened is that Iago is the devil. That's why he's trying to find the cloven hooves that the fables tell us the devil can never disguise, whatever shape he takes. That's why he looks down at Iago's feet. But, of course, Iago isn't a devil; he's a man. Othello and the audience are left confronting the problem of human evil, asking what could motivate a human being to bring such horrible events into being?

Othello finally turns to the other Venetians and says, "Will you, I pray, demand that demi-devil why he hath thus ensnared my mind and body?" He gets no answer. Iago himself says only, "Demand me nothing. What you know, you know. From this time forth I never will speak a word." That's his last line in the play. If Iago gave us no coherent rationale for his malice against Othello at the play's beginning, he'll equally give us no explanation of his destruction at the end. "What you know, you know"—which leaves us asking, what does Othello know at the last? I'd like to take a couple of runs at this question and sandwich between them some consideration of an alternative perspective offered by the speeches of Iago's wife, Desdemona's waiting woman, Emilia in the last act.

Literary critics writing on tragedy often suggest that the extremity of suffering of the tragic protagonist leads to a kind of tragic knowledge, an enlightenment concerning the workings of his or her universe, which makes some kind of sense out of his or her experience. And, indeed, Othello does offer his own final narrative of the significance of his experience—the Othello version, we might call it—and he takes control of his story by providing his own end to it. Addressing the assembled company, he makes his narrative coterminous with the orchestration of his death on his own terms. "Soft you, a word or two before you go. I have done the state some service, and they know it. No more of that. I pray you, in your letters, when you shall these unlucky deeds relate, speak of me as I am. Nothing extenuate, nor set down aught in malice. Then must you speak of one that loved not wisely, but too well. Of one not easily jealous, but, being wrought, perplexed in the extreme. Of one whose hand, like the base Indian, threw a pearl away richer than all his tribe. Of one whose subdued eyes, albeit unused to the melting mood, drop tears as fast as the Arabian trees, their medicinable gum. Set you down this. And say besides that in Aleppo once, where a malignant and a turbaned Turk beat a Venetian and traduced the state, I took by the throat the circumcised dog and smote him—thus." He reclaims his identity as soldier servant of the Venetian state. He ends with a reminiscence of the past, before he even married Desdemona. His action, while in North Africa, in Aleppo, in killing a Turk who assaulted a Venetian and slandered the state of Venice, and even as he describes his action in killing that Turk, thus he impales himself on his own sword.

So, why is he talking in the last minutes of his life about this encounter with a Turk many years ago? We may by now have almost forgotten the presence of the Turks as the enemy menacing Cyprus when the play opened, but they've got a symbolic presence in the language of the play as representative barbaric aliens. It is as if Othello ends by splitting himself into two people, the civilized defender of Venice who kills the savage barbaric alien, and that same alien, for it is himself that the noble Venetian Othello now kills. He murders the murderer that Iago made him into, destroying, purging, exorcizing that aspect of himself. It's also telling that he has already linked himself to another kind of barbaric other from a Eurocentric point of view in his comparison of himself to the Indian who threw away a pearl, just as Othello destroyed his own pearl without price, Desdemona.

Before he arrives at this moment of self-purgation, he first lays out what he feels to be his story, seeking to dictate the terms in which his actions are to be explained and interpreted. To borrow the language of *Hamlet*, he's unfolding himself. He starts by addressing the horrified Venetians who are onstage as his audience, instructing them what they must say of him. Set down this. And then he moves into the third person, offers an illusion of objectivity, again dividing himself, as if sitting in judgment upon another.

First, he says, they must speak of one who loved not wisely, but too well. Too well. He means his love for Desdemona was so great that when he knew her to be false, he could only kill her, because his whole identity was predicated on her virtue and faith. But, loving too well might bear another interpretation. To love too well could also be to forgive all, to show mercy. Why was this kind of love not available to Othello?

He describes himself as one not easily jealous. Does this sum it all up? Not easily jealous, but being wrought, perplexed in the extreme, he says. That verb wrought, here, indicates he's worked upon, even transformed by somebody else. He has become something remade and he thus transfers the moral onus to Iago who has wrought him, manipulated him from his natural state into a madness of jealousy. It's almost as if he is pleading not guilty by reason of insanity, an insanity that is the creation of somebody else. But, in choosing to believe Iago, rather than making a leap of faith and trusting in Desdemona, was he indeed not easily jealous?

Some readers of this play—I include myself among their number—find it terrifying just how easily jealous Othello is. This is not to deny the consummate skill Iago employs in poisoning his mind, but it is to suggest that Iago's machinations are equaled by the terrible vulnerability of Othello to Iago's persuasion, his frightening predisposition to transform Desdemona from goddess into whore. As a contrast to this, listen to Emilia in an impassioned exchange with Othello earlier in the last scene. He has informed her that he has killed Desdemona because of what Iago has told him about her adulterous doings and that his action is not blameworthy. "Oh I were damned beneath all depth in hell but if I did proceed upon just grounds. Thy husband knew it all." Emilia, horrified and bemused, several times repeats blankly, "My husband?" until, eventually, Othello explodes. "He, woman, I say thy husband, dost understand the word? My friend, thy husband, honest, honest Iago." And Emilia explodes back: "If he say so, may his pernicious soul rot half a grain a day. He lies to the heart." And when Othello tries to silence her protestations and threatens violence, she goes on: "Thou hast not half the power to do me harm as I have to be hurt. Oh gull, Oh dolt, as ignorant as dirt."

Even when she's told her own husband has proved Desdemona's guilt, Emilia declares her faith immediately and absolutely for

Desdemona. There is nothing comparable here to Othello's agonizing over the rival claims of Desdemona and Iago's honesty. Emilia's instincts will not let her believe that Desdemona was false. Weighing her against her own husband, she immediately rewrites "honest, honest Iago" as a man with a pernicious soul. Othello has claimed he would be damned if he proceeded on any other than just cause, but Emilia won't accept his self-definition as an agent of divine justice, but calls him "gull"—a fool and a sucker—"dolt, as ignorant as dirt."

Emilia's reward for speaking out, of course, is first to be shouted down by Othello, then to be murdered by her husband. The whole issue of whose voices are heard, believed, acted upon, and validated is crucial in this play. Othello will not hear any of Desdemona's protestations just before he kills her. His smothering of her voice is emphasized even more keenly when Desdemona revives briefly and speaks once more before she is gone for good. "A guiltless death I die," she says. When Emilia asks who has killed her, she says, "Nobody, I myself. Farewell. Commend me to my kind lord." "My kind lord"—she, in effect, forgives Othello, absolves him, tries to save him, but look what happens then.

Othello will have nothing of it. He tells Emilia, "She's like a liar gone to burning hell. 'Twas I that killed her." Othello calls Desdemona a liar who is bound for damnation and, as we've seen, he similarly tries to silence Emilia as she challenges his self-assumed identity of heavenly revenger.

When the other Venetians have come into the room and Emilia reveals that it was she who took the handkerchief and gave it to Iago, Iago's response is to call her a whore, just as Othello has called Desdemona a strumpet when she claimed she never gave Cassio the handkerchief. Tellingly, when Desdemona and Emilia speak what their men don't want to hear, they are labeled whores. As if the openness of one bodily orifice becomes interchangeable with the looseness of the other. Othello kills Desdemona to control her sexuality. Iago kills Emilia to shut her mouth. I should observe at this point that in the 16th century and the 17th century, our society punished women who were thought to talk too much almost as harshly as women convicted of prostitution. Prostitutes were whipped, sometimes even branded. Women convicted of being scolds or nagging wives were locked for hours in horrible iron bridles, called scolds bridles.

Emilia, like Desdemona, dies a selfless death. Desdemona tried to hide her lord's guilt in her final utterance. Emilia, killed by her husband for defending Desdemona's honor, reiterates her lady's innocence in her own last words. "Moor, she was chaste. She loved thee cruel moor. So come my soul to bliss, as I speak true." Their deaths contrast interestingly with the dramatically impressive, shocking, poignant, but absolutely self-centered death of Othello, in which he simultaneously lays claims to the right to write his own history, to explain his actions, and splits himself, as I said before, into the noble Othello and the savage barbaric Othello, the former killing the latter.

In the long speech Othello delivers before he kills himself, no other character in his drama is actually named. Iago isn't mentioned; he is the unnamed person who wrought Othello and made him a killer. Desdemona only appears in the metaphor that makes her the pearl that Othello threw away.

A final thought, in looking at Othello's actions as the play ends, after he has learned of Desdemona's innocence, we might think again of Iago's "What you know, you know," and ask whether Othello ever knows Desdemona truly. Having personified himself, at the start of Act 5, scene 2, as divine justice, he now goes to the other extreme and insists that he is a kind of super sinner, already damned. Looking at the body of his dead wife, he says, "Now how dost thou look now? Oh ill-starred wench, pale as thy smock! When we shall meet at count this look of thine will hurl my soul from heaven, and fiends will snatch at it."

His vision of Desdemona has once again been articulated in black and white terms. She's now utterly pure and utterly separate. She is a supremely virtuous soul who, if they meet again after death, at the day of count—that is, the Day of Judgment—will give him a look that will cast him into eternal damnation. As if she has become a cruel and unforgiving God. Has he heard Desdemona's last loving, forgiving words? Has he heard Emilia's dying confirmation of Desdemona's absolute love for him? "She loved thee, cruel moor," says Emilia. Would love, as embodied in Desdemona, act like that, refusing to forgive, sending the sinning beloved to perdition?

But, Desdemona and Emilia's voices, the voices which testify to Desdemona's love and her forgiveness, go unheard. Othello continues to be locked in his black and white vision in which Desdemona is either black as pitch or so pure she couldn't possibly forgive him. There's a poignant irony here, since as a black-skinned man Othello himself has always been made vulnerable by such a viewpoint, but he can't seem to escape it. Indeed, he dies in those terms, divides himself into enemy alien and noble warrior, another kind of black and white, at the end.

In Othello's imaginative universe, which insists on such extreme oppositions, such schematic dualities, some middle term is missing. I'd suggest to you, it is love.

Lecture Eleven
King Lear I—Kingship and Kinship

Scope:

In *Othello*, much of the play is devoted to the *process* by which its hero makes a destructive choice; *King Lear*, by contrast, explores the *consequences* of the rash choices that Lear makes at the work's beginning. This lecture begins by discussing the love test Lear devises to divide his kingdom between his daughters. It then addresses the implications of the protagonist's double identity as king and father and of the play's entanglement of political action with family strife.

This tragedy offers a double plot in the parallel stories of Lear and his daughters and Gloucester and his sons: two imperceptive fathers fall victim to the machinations of "unnatural" children. After some consideration of the Gloucester plot, the lecture addresses the slippery connotations of the word *nature* within the action of the play and concludes by examining the sequence of events whereby Lear denounces his "unnatural" daughters and alienates himself from the world in which they flourish.

Outline

I. The public dimension of Lear's tragedy is particularly emphasized in this play.

    A. Lear's capricious actions as an old man, facing death and greedy for love, are also those of a king and have national consequences.

    B. The love test that Lear believes will reconfirm his power over his children's lives is to have drastic and far-reaching repercussions.

II. The making of irrevocable choices in this play occurs very early.

    A. As the play opens, Lear rashly and unreflectingly chooses to divide his kingdom, to disinherit and banish the daughter who truly loves him, and to banish his most loyal follower, Kent.

    B. Cordelia's decision not to play Lear's game is equally swift, as is Kent's attack on Lear for his actions toward her.

   C. Cordelia's actions affirm her own sense of the integrity of her love and of the proper duty of a daughter but are interpreted by Lear as disloyal and transgressive.

III. Lear's actions are implicitly and explicitly challenged from the very start.

   A. The king of France makes it clear that Lear is blind to Cordelia's virtues.

   B. Even Cordelia's sisters, who have benefited from Lear's rashness, recognize his folly.

   C. Kent unceremoniously chastises his king: "What wilt thou do old man?... See better, Lear…."

IV. Lear cannot see that he is transforming himself from a king to an impotent old man.

   A. He attempts to retain the title and prerogatives of a monarch, while divesting himself of regal power and royal responsibility.

   B. When he is treated less than respectfully at Goneril's castle, his court Fool points out that he has reversed the parent-child hierarchy and given his older daughters power over him.

   C. This revises the fantasy of being totally loved and indulged by a daughter-turned-mother that had shaped his expectations of Cordelia.

   D. The Fool's constant harping on Lear's own folly eventually provokes Lear's first faint admission that he did Cordelia wrong.

V. *King Lear* has a complex double plot that aligns Lear's relations with his daughters with the Earl of Gloucester's dealings with his sons.

   A. Both men learn to "see better" the hard way, after trusting the wrong children.

   B. Shakespeare juxtaposes Lear's rash choice with Gloucester's credulous response to the illegitimate Edmund's suggestion that Edgar, his legitimate heir, is plotting against him.

   C. Gloucester believes Edgar to have behaved "unnaturally," just as Lear believed Cordelia to have behaved "unnaturally."

VI. The question of what constitutes natural or unnatural behavior in this play may be related to its larger exploration of the very nature of *nature*.

    A. To behave "naturally" in the world of this play is ostensibly to behave in a humane fashion. But the nature of nature is always up for grabs.

    B. When Edmund invokes Nature as his goddess, he opposes her laws to the cultural customs that make him—as an illegitimate (or "natural") son—unable to inherit his father's lands.

    C. Edmund wants to be disencumbered of society's rules and moralities. His nature is a proto-Darwinian nature, knowing no altruism, no ties of loyalty or love.

VII. The inexorable process by which Lear himself is stripped down to a "state of nature" begins with his Act 1 confrontation with Goneril.

    A. Realizing that he no longer has any authority to wield against his daughter, he is increasingly vulnerable to the uncontrollable emotions her "filial ingratitude" arouses in him.

    B. When Goneril asks him to dismiss half of his train of attendants, Lear invokes nature's cruelest powers to punish her for her "unnatural" behavior.

    C. His curse does not strike Goneril, however: it is her father who will suffer most immediately.

    D. Lear's subsequent confrontation with Regan at Gloucester's castle shows that he is still trying to quantify love (in this case, according to how many followers each daughter will allow him).

VIII. When it becomes clear that Regan and Goneril both wish to reduce him to a condition of complete dependency, Lear explodes.

    A. He cries out impotently for revenge but is able neither to articulate what he wishes to do nor to enact it—and he recognizes himself to be on the verge of madness.

B. When he flees to the barren landscape beyond the castle and into a fierce storm, the cruel nature he called down upon Goneril is now raging both within him and without.

Essential Reading:

Shakespeare, *King Lear.*

Questions to Consider:

1. How much responsibility does Cordelia bear for the events of 1.1., and how might you instruct the actress playing this role to behave and speak in this scene?

2. Consider the scenes in which Edmund manipulates Gloucester and Edgar into believing the worst of each other. Do we have another Iago here, or is there something different to be found in Edmund's tactics of persuasion?

Lecture Eleven—Transcript
King Lear I—Kingship and Kinship

Writers who have offered theories of tragedy have often suggested that their tragic protagonists' experience should have a public, as well as a private dimension. Their suffering or fall should not be a matter of just one person coming to grief, but involve or have reverberations within a whole community. In *King Lear*, the public and, indeed, national reverberations of Lear's actions are made clear from the first. His every decision, however personal and capricious, has the potential to affect his whole kingdom. Lear, as king, has two identities. He's a monarch with no sons and three daughters, who must decide who is to inherit his kingdom and because two of those daughters already have powerful husbands, which of the potential factions in that kingdom he will favor. But, he's also an old man, facing death, greedy for love. As the play opens, he is about to enact a plan that seems designed to reconfirm his power over his children's lives and affections. Its consequences will be more drastic and far-reaching than he has ever dreamed.

I've noted before that the act of choosing is often a crucial component of tragic drama. Think back to *Hamlet* and *Othello* where, in different ways, the process of choosing became central to the action. We see Hamlet endlessly reflecting on his situation and reviewing his options. We see the gradual poisoning of Othello's mind and his agonized articulation of his dilemma to Iago. "I think my wife be honest, and think she is not, I think that thou art just, and think thou art not." Whom is he to trust? There's no equivalent of this in *King Lear*, no agonized self-interrogation, no preliminary soliloquy; Lear acts violently and irrationally from the first. Within a single scene, he makes a series of disastrous choices. He chooses to divide his kingdom and let go the reins of power. He chooses to disinherit Cordelia, the one daughter who really loves him. He chooses to banish his most loyal follower, the earl of Kent.

Other people's choices are no less swift. Cordelia has only a couple of brief asides before she shows Lear she won't play his game. Kent doesn't pause before he attacks Lear for rejecting Cordelia. The action of this play will focus much less on the process of choosing than upon the consequences of choices and especially the far-reaching and devastating consequences of the choices Lear makes at the very start.

We begin Act 1 with a love test that is rather reminiscent of something out of a folk or fairy tale. There is, indeed, a folktale in which a king asks his daughter to say how much she loves him and banishes her for her apparent callous impertinence when she says she loves him as much as meat loves salt. Later, in disguise as a kitchen maid, she presents him with a tasteless unsalted dish of meat and her father weeps as he realizes what his apparently lost daughter meant.

Lear claims that his children will win their inheritance in proportion to how successfully they demonstrate their love, but his test is fixed from the start. Although it seems as if the daughters are to win Lear's bounty in proportion to their loving speeches, when after Goneril and Regan have spoken, Lear turns to Cordelia, he says: "What can you say to draw a third more opulent than your sisters? Speak." Lear expects his favorite to do best and he has already set aside the most generous portion for her. But Cordelia, who is never going to win the Miss Congeniality award, refuses to follow Lear's script, refuses to quantify her love. Love, for her, has nothing to do with staged declarations. We've already guessed what will happen because of the remarks she has made aside. When Goneril has finished declaring her love, Cordelia sadly remarks, "What shall Cordelia speak? Love, and be silent." And after Regan's protestations, Cordelia declares, "I'm sure my love's more ponderous than my tongue. It's more substantial than any words I could give to it."

So, we are less surprised than Lear when in answer to his question she offers her resounding, "Nothing, my lord" and then qualifies her denial. "I cannot heave my heart into my mouth. I love your majesty according to my bond, no more, no less." According to my bond. What is her bond? How does she define her filial duty? Well, she does so by addressing what is problematic within her sister's lavish declarations:

> "Good my lord, you have begot me, bred me, loved me. I
> return those duties back as are right fit, obey you, love you,
> and most honor you. Why have my sisters husbands, if they
> say they love you all? Haply, when I shall wed, that lord
> whose hand must take my plight shall carry half my love
> with him, half my care and duty. Sure, I shall never marry
> like my sisters, to love my father all."

©2007 The Teaching Company.

She speaks to the loyalties of women who are expected by their society to switch their allegiance from father to husband. You may recall Desdemona made a similar argument to her father when he asked her to whom she owed her duty. What are my married sisters doing, Cordelia says, insisting that all their love is still placed in their father?

As in *Othello*, we have a play which starts out with an action by a young woman that her father chooses to construe as an unnatural act, a transgression. Lear's response is swift and terrible. You might also note its utter selfishness. "Better thou hadst not been born than not to have pleased me better." I'm struck by the fact that Lear doesn't say you should have loved me better, but rather you should have pleased me better. We should note at once a big difference between the world of *Hamlet* and that of *Lear*. Nobody in Denmark, except Hamlet, seems to have been especially disturbed by Claudius's hasty marriage to Gertrude, but the first scene of *Lear* is full of implicit and explicit critiques of Lear's action.

Cordelia's suitor, the king of France, declares, "Fairest Cordelia, that art most rich, being poor, most choice, forsaken, and most loved, despised. Thee and thy virtues here I seize upon. Be it lawful I take up what's cast away." While not directly addressing Lear, he makes it quite clear that he thinks Lear doesn't realize what a jewel he's throwing away in Cordelia. Even Goneril and Regan, who have benefited from Lear's rashness, recognize his folly. "He always loved our sister most, and with what poor judgment he hath now cast her off, appears too grossly," says Goneril, and Regan responds, "He hath ever but slenderly known himself." This is not a man who has ever reflected carefully on his own actions.

Then, of course, there is the outspoken earl of Kent. "Thy youngest daughter does not love thee least," bellows Kent. "Nor are those empty hearted whose low sounds reverb no hollowness," and later on, "See better, Lear." Kent has already explained his lack of ceremony on the grounds that his very uncourtly criticism is excused by the craziness of Lear's action. "Let Kent be unmannerly," he says, "when Lear is mad. What wilt thou do, old man?"

It's telling that Kent, with astonishing bluntness, addresses the king as "old man" because this is to be Lear's essential identity from now on, the identity he must learn to come to terms with. To be sure, Lear still believes he can order things on his own terms. Speaking to the husbands of Goneril and Regan, the dukes of Albany and Cornwall, he says:

> "I do invest you jointly with my power, preeminence, and all the large effects that troop with majesty. Our self, by monthly course, with reservation of a hundred knights, by you to be sustained, shall our abode make with you by due turns. Only, we still retain the name and all the additions to a king. The sway, revenue, execution of the rest, beloved sons, be yours."

He speaks with the royal "we," as he tries to achieve the impossible. Retain the title and prerogatives of the monarch, while divesting himself of both regal power and regal responsibility. He wants the name of king, even as he reduces his support base to a train of one hundred knights. In reality, he risks being no more than a dependent old man, an old man who has trusted his welfare to those who are not likely to obey the contract he is drawing up, and Lear very quickly finds this out. Staying at Goneril's castle, he suspects her servants aren't treating him very deferentially. He asks her steward Oswald, "Who am I, sir?" Who the hell do you think I am? "My lady's father," says the man, not "my king."

Lear's court jester, his fool, suggests matters are even worse. The fool has been singing snippets of songs that seem to mock the folly of Lear's actions. When Lear asks, "When were you won't to be so full of songs, sirrah?" The fool replies, "Ever since thou madest thy daughters, thy mother, when thou gavest them the rod and pullst down thine own britches."

Lear has reversed the usual parent-child hierarchy. This reverberates rather interestingly against what Lear himself says petulantly about Cordelia after he has banished her. "I loved her most and sought to set my rest on her kind nursery." That is, I thought to live out my old age in her care. "Nursery" is here the loving care of a nursing mother. His fantasy of being totally loved and indulged by a daughter turned mother is transformed into the reality of heartless daughters who'll treat him like an unloved child.

Lear's fool is, in fact, a very wise fool. Like Kent, he is a loyal critic. Under the cover of the teasing speeches, songs, and jokes of the professional jester, he keeps tossing back to Lear the implications of his actions. Let's take another look at the fool in Act 1, scene 4. When Lear tells Goneril she's looking much too bad tempered, the fool says, "Thou was a pretty fellow when thou hadst no need to care for her frowning. I am better than thou art now. I am a fool, thou art nothing." Nothing is, of course, a word that reverberates through this play.

And finally, when Lear storms out of Goneril's castle to seek out Regan's home, convinced she will be more loving and dutiful than her sister, the fool points out his error. "Regan is a twin to Goneril," he suggests, "they're as alike as two crabapples,"—two sour apples. In the scene of rather hard-edged banter that follows, there's an odd moment when Lear, out of nowhere, says, "I did her wrong." He doesn't follow up or explain this statement, but it is as if, just for a moment, he confronts the mistake he has made in disowning Cordelia.

I now want to return to Kent's remark, "See better, Lear." There are, in fact, two old men in this play who have to learn how to see properly: Lear and one of his noblemen, the earl of Gloucester. One will go mad before he sees clearly again, and one will literally lose his eyes before he gains any insight. Shakespeare creates a double plot. We have two stories of fathers who choose to trust the wrong children, who can't see where love really lies. The play offers theme and variation. The parallel is structurally brought to our attention because the scene in which Lear makes all his crucial choices is framed by two episodes involving Gloucester and his children.

The play begins in a leisurely manner, as two noblemen, Kent and Gloucester, speculate on the king's intentions and one of them introduces his son to the other. Gloucester's son, Edmund, was born out of wedlock. His older and legitimate brother, Edgar, will inherit Gloucester's lands. Gloucester explains the situation with a kind of shamefaced bravado:

> "I have, sir, a son by order of law, some year elder than this, who yet is no dearer in my account, though this knave came somewhat saucily into the world before he was sent for, yet was his mother fair. There was good sport at his making, and the whoreson must be acknowledged."

Gloucester is both tactless and complacent, as he jokes about Edmund's origins, and all the time Edmund stands there and hardly says a word. But, if Edmund is almost silent here, he gets the first soliloquy in the play, just like Iago does in *Othello*. You might want to think about whether there are other similarities between Edmund and Iago. Edmund's certainly just as much a skeptic about other people's conventional notions of wisdom and virtue, and he is equally adept at masking his real nature.

Edmund will successfully manipulate Gloucester into believing the legitimate son, Edgar, has been plotting against Gloucester's life. He cleverly makes Edgar keep out of Gloucester's way so that they'll never get together and clarify matters between them. In Act 2, he persuades his father that he was wounded by Edgar for refusing to help his brother murder their father, and even as he poison's Gloucester's mind, Edgar is fleeing the castle, still believing Edmund is on his side.

Edmund discloses the supposedly criminal Edgar's unnatural purpose to kill his father and Gloucester embraces him, calling him his loyal and natural son. Note the pun here; a natural son is, in Shakespeare's time, the polite way of referring to a son born out of wedlock. Now the natural son is declared the truly natural son, the one who has behaved with proper filial loyalty. The opposition between natural and unnatural keeps recurring. Gloucester and Lear decide that Edgar and Cordelia are unnatural children and then choose to favor other children who eventually teach them what it is really like to have a really unnatural child.

Natural, unnatural—the word nature, with all its derivatives, reverberates through *King Lear*. It's a very slippery term and it is constantly under negotiation in the play. Nature can mean "Nature" with a capital N, the natural world that may or may not reflect a divine order of things. It can also, of course, mean human nature, inner nature, where to be natural is to be humane. The old word for nature is, in fact, "kind," "kind" in Middle English. To behave kindly is to behave naturally. But, the very notion of nature is always being constructed by human beings, even if they may believe that nature is in some sense prior to the culture that decides what constitutes nature. Also, it means different things to different people in the play, which brings me back to Edmund's soliloquy at the start of Act 1, scene 2:

"Thou, nature, art my goddess. To thy law my services are bound. Wherefore should I stand in the plague of custom, and permit the curiosity of nations to deprive me, for that I am some 12 or 14 moonshines lag of a brother? Why bastard? Wherefore base? When my dimensions are as well compact, my mind as generous, and my shape as true, as honest madam's issue... As to the legitimate—fine word, legitimate. Well, my legitimate, if this letter speed, and my invention thrive, Edmund, the base, shall top the legitimate. I grow; I prosper. Now, gods, stand up for bastards."

When Edmund invokes nature as his patron goddess, he opposes her in effect to those curious and petty cultural social and legal practices, which make him illegitimate, which call him bastard and baseborn. The irony in this play, of course, is that Edmund, the bastard, is a real bastard. He scorns custom, tradition, the arbitrary and idiosyncratic rules of society, both the discrepancy between the way the legitimate and illegitimate sons are treated and the very fact that the firstborn must always inherit an estate under the law of primogeniture.

You might want to note that the English law was pretty tough on bastard children in Shakespeare's time. A father might make separate provision for illegitimate children, but they had no automatic claims on the parental estate. Indeed, even legitimate younger sons suffered considerably under a system that gave the lion's share of an inheritance to the firstborn male.

Edmund believes that we should follow our own natural appetites, just as his own father had followed his in begetting Edmund. He wants to be disencumbered from society's rules and moralities. Of course, he is appropriating the notion of nature for his own purposes, ignoring that other sense of natural, which would declare it to be utterly unnatural to be plotting against his own kin. Edmund's nature is a proto Darwinian nature, red in tooth and claw, knowing no altruism, no ties of loyalty or love, where only the most ruthless survive.

But, that is yet to come. In Acts 1 and 2, we see the beginnings of the stripping down of Lear himself to the state of nature, after he divests himself of the power, which should back up his kingly identity. His altered condition becomes evident in his arguments with Goneril and

Regan about his personal retinue of one hundred knights. Lear begins to realize he no longer has any authority to wield against his daughters. He also feels increasingly powerless against the uncontrollable emotions their filial ingratitudes arouse in him, emotions which threaten to drive him insane. If Lear at times seems to be overreacting to his daughters' behavior, remember that at this time there was a much greater weight on public respect to be paid to parents by children. Even adult children were expected to behave with extreme deference to their parents. There's absolutely no equivalent in Renaissance England to the teenager, who, like, rolls their eyes at whatever the parent says.

In his confrontation with Goneril, when she asks him sweetly to send away half of the knights who attend on him, there's a moment of feline unmasking when she makes it clear that she is currently politely requesting what she already has the power to enforce without his approval. How can he stop her, if she chooses to banish half his followers? What army will now do his will? Lear's response is to curse her and his speech, like Edmund's, invokes the goddess Nature herself: "Hear, Nature, hear. Dear goddess, hear. Suspend thy purpose, if thou didst intend to make this creature fruitful. Into her womb convey sterility."

Lear invokes Nature's cruelest powers. Goneril has been an unnatural child. He asks that Mother Nature deprive Goneril of her power to be a mother. Later on, in his diatribe, he begs that if Goneril does give birth, Nature should make her child an unnatural torment to its mother, so that his daughter may learn how sharper than a serpent's tooth it is to have a thankless child. But, this is a play in which people are always calling on the gods, on various cosmic forces, and it is not at all clear that anybody is out there listening. Lear's curse doesn't strike Goneril. It's he who will suffer most immediately, both inwardly and outwardly, from Nature's cruelties.

Lear storms out of Goneril's home to seek refuge with Regan, still blind to the fact that Regan and Goneril are pretty much alike. He ends up at Gloucester's castle. He doesn't himself even get to enter the fortress, but rather has a bitter confrontation with Regan, who with her husband is already in residence there and with Goneril, who has followed her father to run her own intervention.

Regan speaks the same language as Goneril did. You are an old man, you should be ruled by others; you are not king anymore. Their confrontation climaxes with another battle over the numbers in Lear's retinue. Goneril said he must dismiss fifty of his knights. Regan goes further. "If you will come to me, for now I spy a danger, I entreat you to bring but five and twenty. To no more will I give place or notice." And her father says, "I gave you all." "And in good time you gave it." "Made you my guardians, my depositories, but kept a reservation to be followed with such a number. What, must I come to you with five and twenty, Regan? Said you so?" "And speak it again, my lord; no more with me." Lear turns at this point to Goneril and says, "I'll go with thee, thy fifty yet doth double five and twenty, and thou art twice her love."

There's something tremendously poignant about this exchange. In his blindness, Lear still tries to quantify love, as he did in the disastrous love test. Here he measures love according to how many followers each daughter will allow him. Although perhaps it is not ultimately the numbers that are at issue here, but rather what keeping his knights would represent—his kingly authority, his sense of his own identity as regal father, the affirmation of his daughters obedience to the social contract he drew up earlier.

And this is what happens. Goneril says, "Hear me, my lord. What need you five and twenty, ten, or five, to follow in a house where twice so many have a command to tend you?" "What need one," adds Regan. And then, Lear, maddened with fury and his own sense of powerlessness, explodes: "You see me here, you gods, a poor old man, as full of grief as age, wretched in both. If it be you that stir these daughters' hearts against their father, fool me not so much to bear it tamely. Touch me with noble anger, and let not women's weapons, water drops, stain my man's cheeks. No, you unnatural hags, I will have such revenges on you both, that all the world shall—I will do such things—what they are, yet I know not, but they shall be the terrors of the earth. You think I'll weep. No, I'll not weep. I have full cause of weeping. But this heart shall break into a hundred thousand flaws, or ere I'll weep. Oh fool, I shall go mad."

On the verge of insanity, he leaves the castle, goes out into the night and wind and rain. He storms off into the same cruel Nature he called down upon Goneril. Now, it rages both inside him and outside. The play enacts a brutal dynamic by which the expulsion and rejection of a child is followed by the expulsion and rejection of the father who disowned her. Lear rejected both honest love and honest service. Now, he is naked to the elements.

Lecture Twelve
King Lear II—"Unaccommodated Man"

Scope:

This lecture focuses on Shakespeare's interest in the stripping and refashioning of identities in Act 3 of *King Lear*. Edgar, disowned by his father and disguised as a crazed beggar, and Lear, driven insane by his older daughters' callousness and ingratitude, collide with Kent, Gloucester, and Lear's Fool in a chaotic night on a storm-swept heath. Wild and fragmentary interchanges between these lost or alienated figures produce a kind of theater of the absurd in which Lear rages at the storm and attempts to solve the enigma of evil itself: "Is there any cause in nature that makes these hard hearts?" The lecture explores the idiosyncratic dramatic juxtapositions and oppositions out of which Shakespeare creates his new society of fools and madmen; it also sketches out some of the larger questions that are forced upon Lear and Gloucester by the extremity of their suffering.

Outline

I. In the middle portion of *Lear*, Shakespeare puts several of his characters through a purgatorial stripping down and refashioning of their identities.

   A. The expulsions and rejections of children are followed by the expulsion and rejection of the fathers who disowned them.

   B. Edgar, fleeing the manhunt provoked by Edmund's machinations, takes on the disguise of a half-naked beggar and renames himself "Poor Tom."

   C. Edmund's plotting causes Gloucester to be accused of treason by Cornwall: his eyes are put out, and he is expelled from his own castle.

II. As disguised, dispossessed, and maddened characters collide with one another on the heath, Shakespeare emphasizes the confusion created by their obsessive and solipsistic behavior.

   A. Lear, in his madness, asks the storm to smite his enemies but also indicts it as an agent of his cruel daughters; he is absolutely fixated upon their "filial ingratitude."

B. Shakespeare crafts some particularly bitter dramatic ironies in juxtaposing Gloucester's remarks about ungrateful children with the remarks of his own banished son.

   1. Gloucester's blindness to Edmund's scheming is echoed in his inability to see through Edgar's disguise.

   2. Only when he is literally blinded will Gloucester receive the information that will force him to "see" that Edgar was slandered.

III. Lear's obsession with the sins of Goneril and Regan consumes his being.

   A. On seeing Poor Tom's wretched state, he assumes that he has been beggared by his daughters.

   B. In a hut on the heath, he has the supposed mad beggar and his own fool preside over a surreal mock arraignment of Goneril and Regan.

   C. Lear's preoccupation with his ill treatment extends to a desire to anatomize the origins of evil itself: "Is there any cause in nature that makes these hard hearts?"

IV. Lear is also fascinated by Poor Tom, the Bedlam beggar.

   A. For Lear, Tom's near-naked and self-mutilated body represents humanity stripped bare of all trappings of civilization (in contrast to his daughters, whose rich clothes and beauty hid their bestial natures).

   B. The sight of Tom reinforces Lear's earlier meditations in the storm about the vulnerability of the poorest in society to nature's cruelties.

V. Lear and Gloucester make related, but not identical, physical and spiritual journeys through the night.

   A. Lear is punished for his errors with insanity; Gloucester's physical blinding repays his failure to see clearly.

   B. Lear's aggressive madness and his defiance of the elements are inverted in Gloucester's despairing vision of human beings as the playthings of uncaring gods.

   C. Gloucester asks that Poor Tom guide him toward Dover (where he has already dispatched Lear to meet Cordelia's invading forces). From the convergence on Dover Beach of two erring old men, Shakespeare will make one of the most powerful pieces of theater ever written.

Essential Reading:

Shakespeare, *King Lear.*

Supplementary Reading:

Dollimore, *Radical Tragedy*, chapter 13.

Questions to Consider:

1. Why does Shakespeare devote so many lines to Kent's acrimonious confrontation with Cornwall and Oswald before Lear arrives at Gloucester's castle?

2. King Lear falls into madness; Edgar pretends to be deranged. Is the language of their (real or pretended) insanity at all similar to that used by Hamlet when adopting his "antic disposition"?

Lecture Twelve—Transcript
King Lear II—"Unaccommodated Man"

At the end of Act 2, Lear storms off into the same cruel nature he called down upon Goneril. Now, the destructive power of nature rages both inside him and outside him. As I've already suggested, the play enacts a brutal dynamic by which the expulsions and rejections of children—Cordelia, Edgar—are followed by the rejection and expulsion of the fathers who disowned them. The same night, in this same castle, Edmund will gain the information, which will allow him to usurp his father's place.

In the middle portion of the play, Shakespeare puts several of his characters through a kind of purgatorial stripping down and refashioning of their identities. The mad King Lear has been sent into Nature at its cruelest. But, we have already had this situation anticipated in the fate of Gloucester's legitimate son Edgar, framed by his half-brother Edmund so that he appears to have been plotting to usurp his father's place while Gloucester yet lives.

Edgar has already fled in fear of his life, even before Gloucester formally disowns and banishes him. We see him alone in the wild in Act 2, scene 3, a hunted outlaw. Having lost his noble rank, having been disinherited and exiled, and with the hounds on his trail, he is now stripping himself of all that remains of his former identity:

> "While I may 'scape, I will preserve myself and am bethought to take the basest and most poorest shape that ever penury, in contempt of man, brought near to beast. My face I'll grime with filth, blanket my loins, elf all my hair in knots. And with presented nakedness out face the winds and persecutions of the sky. The country gives me proof and precedent of bedlam beggars, who, with roaring voices, strike in their numbed and mortified bare arms, pins, wooden pricks, nails, sprigs of rosemary. Poor Turlygod! Poor Tom! That's something yet. Edgar, I nothing am."

Edgar, in his own way, seems to be going back to Nature, a brutally harsh natural world in which wander bedlam beggars, half-naked, half-crazed, homeless vagabonds who mutilate themselves to win charity from those they meet. He says, "Edgar, I nothing am." (I am no more Edgar, but also, as Edgar, I am nothing.) There's perhaps a faint echo here of the fool telling Lear he had made himself nothing.

Edgar has remade himself as the lowest of the low, a crazed beggar ("Poor Tom.") This process of at once stripping off one's identity and transforming oneself has indeed been seen even earlier in the play when Kent shows up in disguise at the start of Act 1, scene 4, so that he may loyally continue to serve his king. In a brief soliloquy, he comments, "I razed my likeness" (I erased my likeness. I razed off my likeness)—presumably by shaving off his beard.

There's one other character who will have his identity erased and transformed. In Act 3, not so very long after disinherited Edgar, seeking to escape his father's vengeance, has become Poor Tom the bedlam beggar, Gloucester himself is going to undergo a terribly similar experience. Edmund, who is very good at manipulating paper trails, uses one letter to frame his brother and another to ruin his father, to make Cornwall, Regan's husband and Gloucester's overlord, turn against him. The letter, described to him in confidence by his father, concerns a faction in England that is now working with Cordelia, who by marriage is queen of France, to reclaim Lear's rights from the incursions of his daughters. So, in the background of the very personal sufferings of the various wanderers in the storm, larger political upheavals are taking place. Once Edmund suggests that Gloucester is in cahoots with the French invaders, and when it becomes known that Gloucester has gone into the storm to offer comfort to Lear against Cornwall's orders, the duke declares Gloucester a traitor. He gives his rank and lands to Edmund, and in one of the most terrible scenes in Shakespeare's plays, Cornwall himself puts out Gloucester's eyes. Expelled from his own castle, Gloucester experiences in reality the condition Edgar has taken upon himself as a disguise—blinded, homeless, he's reduced to a mutilated beggar.

In Acts 3 and 4 Shakespeare will take Gloucester and Lear on brutal journeys that finally bring them together on the beach at Dover, near to the mustering point of Cordelia's invading forces. For now, however, I want to look at the storm scenes on the heath that precede this meeting, scenes in which the play's dramatic structure offers a series of moving, ironic, and even horrific collisions between people and between different perspectives. Shakespeare organizes the wild wanderings of his characters like a complex orchestral score. I'm going to focus now on some of the play's suggestive juxtapositions and also examine the obsessions that drive Lear himself.

So, let's just catalog the people who are wandering this brutal terrain of the storm-swept heath. We have a dispossessed, deranged king, Lear. We have a disguised lord; he banished Kent. We have a king's fool. We have a dispossessed son disguised as a beggar who claims to be possessed by demons, Edgar, and we have the father who banished that son, Gloucester—two men in disguise, a madman, a fool, and an unseeing father who is soon to be blinded in reality. All of them are stumbling around in the darkness and storm in which Gloucester does not recognize Kent and no one has any idea that the mad beggar is Edgar. Lear insists that Edgar, too, has been reduced to the state he's in by cruel daughters and Edgar, in his mad beggar disguise, is quite likely to call the other men by the names of demons and evil spirits.

The characters' ignorance of each other and their fragmentary conversations—conversations in which speakers often pursue their own obsessions or role play in surreal ways—all of these suggest a world gone crazy, full of anarchy and confusion in which everyone is locked in the prison house of his own fears or fantasies or resentments. Let's start with Lear, raging against the elements:

> "Blow, winds, and crack your cheeks. Rage, blow. You cataracts and hurricanoes, spout till you have drenched our steeples, drowned the cocks. And thou, all shaking thunder, smite flat the thick rotundity of the world. Crack nature's moulds, all germens spill at once, that make ingrateful man."

He begins by challenging forces of nature to do their worst to him and to smite his enemies and to destroy everything in the universe that goes to produce the forces of ingratitude that have driven him over the edge. Then, still addressing the forces of the storm, he upbraids the cruel agents or ministers of Nature for seeming to be at the service of his cruel daughters, for all too conveniently producing a storm to supplement the women's spite. Invoking the elements he says, "Here I stand, your slave, a poor, infirm, weak, and despised old man, but yet I call you servile ministers, that have with two pernicious daughters joined your high engendered battles against a head so old and white as this."

The very forces of nature, he claims, are now in league with his pernicious daughters. But, later on, when Kent is begging him to take shelter in a hovel he has found, Lear declares himself immune to the elements because the storm outside can do nothing to him in comparison with the storm in his own being. "Thou thinkst 'tis much that this contentious storm invades us to the skin. So it is to thee, but where the greater malady is fixed, the lesser is scarce felt...The tempest in my mind doth from my senses take all feeling else save what beats there. Filial ingratitude. Is it not as this mouth should tear this hand for lifting food to it? But I will punish home. No, I will weep no more. In such a night to shut me out. Pour on. I will endure. In such a night as this. Oh Regan, Goneril. Your old, kind father, whose frank heart gave all—That way madness lies; let me shun that; no more of that."

His image of a mouth tearing at its own hand for giving it food, of a body at war against itself, suggests his horror at realizing that his daughters, the flesh of his own flesh, are not indeed under his control, and not continuous with his own will. He has assumed that, like extensions of himself, they would do his bidding. They turn out not only to be utterly separate from his will, but to be his antagonists, and he is absolutely fixated upon what has been done to him. It consumes his world. He rages at his own impotence, and as he agonizes over his daughters' cruelty, he's all too aware of the insanity that's about to possess him.

And woven into the spectacle of Lear descending into madness are other collisions in the dark. The hovel proves to be inhabited by Poor Tom, the crazed beggar who is constantly babbling of the fiend he says torments him, when Gloucester turns up, pursuing Lear on his personal rescue mission, a lone man brandishing a lighted torch in the darkness. Edgar—Edgar as Tom—cries out, "This is the foul fiend Flibbertigibbet." Edgar, acting in character as the mad beggar, insists this new arrival is some night-walking demon, but for us, it's as if he is all too accurately venting his pain on the father who has behaved like a capricious devil to him.

The ironies of the situation are compounded when Gloucester speaks to Lear. He compares the cruelty of Lear's daughters to what he thinks he knows about Edgar's treachery. "Our flesh and blood is grown so vile, my lord that it doth hate what gets it." He speaks of our own flesh and blood hating the person who begets it, fathers it, even as his son Edgar raves next to him. Gloucester seems to be doomed to say things that are rendered bitterly ironic by circumstances of which he is ignorant. He will later refer to the warnings of the man he calls, "poor banished Kent," while the disguised Kent is standing at his side. But, at present, his mind is on his own apparently ungrateful child. "I had a son," Gloucester goes on, "now outlawed from my blood. He sought my life, but lately, very late, I loved him, friend. No father his son dearer. Truth tell thee, the grief have crazed my wits."

His report that Edgar's actions, or at least the actions he thinks Edgar has carried out, have crazed his wits gives us a doubling of Lear's own condition with the extra twist that the same Edgar then says, "Tom's a-cold." This is to be his repeated refrain, "Tom's a-cold." Edgar, of course, is practically naked to the storm, but also presumably chilled to the bone by his father's hasty judgment upon him, the father who has not seen and will not yet see.

Of course, Edgar's wretchedness in this scene is counterbalanced later by Gloucester's own agony. A few scenes later, bound and tortured and blinded by Cornwall and his henchmen, Gloucester calls out for help from the son he thinks loves him. "All dark and comfortless, where's my son Edmund? Edmund," he declares, "will revenge him." And it is then that Cornwall reveals that it was Edmund who betrayed his confidence.

Gloucester learns the truth, sees what has really been happening at the very moment that Cornwall plucks out his eyes. "Oh my follies!" he says. "Then, Edgar was abused." Edgar was slandered; Edgar was framed.

If Edgar, on the heath, pretends to be possessed by various demons, Lear is obsessed by the ingratitude of his daughters. He's monomaniacal on the subject. When he sees Edgar for the first time, his first words are, "Hast thou given all to thy two daughters? And hast thou come to this? Couldst thou save nothing? Didst thou give them all?"

His obsession climaxes in the mock arraignment of his own daughters in Act 3, scene 6—a trial at which he makes the mad beggar and his own fool the presiding justices. Lear makes his deposition in a kind of parody of legal procedure. "Arraign her first, 'tis Goneril, I here take my oath before this honorable assembly, she kicked the poor king, her father." But, even as they stage a mock trial, Lear wants to go further than merely putting somebody to the question. In the midst of the very, very black comedy of the scene—

in which Lear's obsessions, and Poor Tom's ravings, and the fool's wry jokes are all jostling together, and Edgar is offering an occasional remark aside in his own identity and can barely hold back his tears—in the middle of all this, Lear hits upon the nub of the matter. "Let them anatomize Regan," he says. "See what breeds about her heart. Is there any cause in nature that makes these hard hearts?"

I should note, parenthetically, that Shakespeare is upping the level of irony even higher here. In the throes of his obsession, Lear does not acknowledge his own hardheartedness, the callousness with which he cast off his best loved daughter, Cordelia. But, in his madness on the heath, he wants to anatomize Regan, not just to explore her actions philosophically or judicially, but to dissect her out to find just what it is that renders her so unfeeling, to find a scientific explanation for what it is in human nature that makes people behave so cruelly to one another. At the time of this play's writing, we actually have the beginnings of empirical science, when medical researchers are publishing new volumes showing their detailed anatomies of the human body. But, Lear wants to go further, beyond bones and muscles and nerves. Why do human beings behave so appallingly to other human beings? What lies at the root of their evil? It is, of course, a version of the question Othello asks of Iago in the last scene of his tragedy, but this is only Act 3 of this play. Lear will have much more time to worry away at the problem.

Even before Lear attempts to put his older daughters on trial, he has become more and more fascinated with Edgar, as he plays out his role as Poor Tom, the bedlam beggar. Edgar is enduring the storm almost naked. The fool jokes that Tom's hypothetical daughters have at least left him a blanket or we'd have all been shamed. The beggar is stripped to his skin. Edgar's playing the role of a crazed pauper, the worst kind of beggar, the kind of beggar you pay to go away when he thrusts his deformities in your face. And in disguise as Poor Tom, Edgar offers a vision of humanity, at its nearest to animal existence. Lear asks Tom what he's been before he fell into beggary. Edgar, elaborating on his new and fictional identity, replies he was a serving man at court who lied and deceived and fornicated with the best of them. He goes on to describe himself: "false of heart, light of ear, bloody of hand, hog in sloth, fox in stealth, wolf in greediness, dog in madness, lion in prey." Of course, he's now reduced to something like the state of the beasts to which he compares himself.

Lear has been obsessed with the bestiality of his daughters. They are supercivilized court ladies on the surface, well groomed, richly dressed, yet behave like animals to him. When Lear is raging at Goneril, he calls her a serpent, a wolf, a vulture. He later describes Goneril and Regan as being "dog-hearted," tigers, not daughters. Now, Lear is confronted with a human being who is visually barely distinguishable from an animal. "Is man no more than this?" he asks. "Consider him well. Thou owest the worm no silk, the beast no hide, the sheep no wool, the cat no perfume. Ha! Here's three of us, sophisticated. Thou art the thing itself. Unaccommodated man is no more, but such a poor bare, forked animal as thou art."

"Unaccommodated man"—man stripped bare of all the trappings of civilization. Lear, in his own frenzy, wants to join Poor Tom in this stripped down state. Addressing his own garments, he says, "Off, off, you lendings." He has to be stopped from stripping himself. But, with or without clothes, Lear himself is pretty near to this stripped down naked state. His royalty won't protect him from the elements. He and we are forcibly reminded of humanity's vulnerability once the fragile protections of civilization are taken away. The sight of Edgar also reinforces a lesson Lear has already begun to learn in the storm. Before the encounter with Edgar, we see Lear, brooding on the cruelties of nature, for perhaps the first time in the play thinking of someone other than himself:

> "Poor naked wretches, where so ever you are, that bide the pelting of this pitiless storm. How shall your houseless heads and unfed sides, your looped and windowed raggedness, defend you from seasons such as these? Oh, I have taken too little care of this. Take physic, pomp. Expose thyself to feel what wretches feel, that thou mayst shake the superflux to them and show the heavens more just."

Take physic pomp. The rich and powerful who live in pomp and pride should take physic, should medicate themselves, by exposing themselves to what the lowest members of society experience. Only such an experience will provoke them to behave more justly to such wretches by giving them some of their own "superflux," their superfluous possessions. This is one of the speeches in *Lear*, which

©2007 The Teaching Company.

explains why the play was actually rather popular in Soviet Russia, as it could be—the speech could be—seen as a sermon on the need for the redistribution of wealth.

Let's return now to the separate paths trod by Lear and Gloucester. Although buffeted by the storm, Lear's sufferings are primarily psychological. His punishments for his errors occur in the turmoil and agony of his mind. Gloucester's punishment is ultimately inscribed upon his body. He failed to see clearly; he loses his eyes in most brutal way. Cornwall has this terrible line as he squeezes them out, "Out, vile jelly." Then, he says, "Let him smell his way to Dover." One of the most frightening productions of the scene actually did not show the eye putting-out on stage. It was happening just off stage, but a group of servants are watching it happen, and you saw the agony and the misery on their faces reflect what was happening to their master.

At the start of Act 4 the blinded Gloucester, thrown out of his own castle, tells the old servant, who is trying to care for him, to leave. But, you cannot see your way, the man says, and Gloucester replies, "I have no way and therefore want no eyes. I stumbled when I saw."

There's a poignant despair in his words "I have no way." His knowledge of what he has done to Edgar deprives him of any sense of a path to follow, a future to enter into. He has, at the same time, lost any sense that he is making his way through a meaningful or just universe. Brooding on what he has learned of Edmund's betrayals he declares, "As flies to wanton boys are we to the gods, they kill us for their sport."

He imagines a universe full of uncaring deities, where human beings are just playthings to be tormented by cruel gods, gods who are as capricious and uncaring as little boys pulling the wings off flies. Certainly, the heavens don't seem in any great hurry to intervene to help either Gloucester or Lear. But, of course, it's more complicated than this. Gloucester has also implied his own culpability, his own responsibility for his plight. "I stumbled when I saw." He, after all, chose to trust Edmund rather than Edgar. But, faced with the horrors of his condition and his knowledge that he has so wronged Edgar, he despairs.

Like Lear, he has become fascinated by the vision of human wretchedness summoned up by the mad beggar, Poor Tom, he met on the heath. This seems to explain why he asks his servant that this same Poor Tom now be his escort as he goes into exile. But, even as he unwittingly requests the help of his own loving son, he hints that further existence would be unthinkable. He begs his new guide Tom to take him to the edge of the great chalk cliffs of Dover beach. "From that place I shall need no leading need." He intends self-extinction.

Gloucester's last action on the heath had been to make arrangements for Lear to travel to Dover in the hope that he could be united there with those who still love and support him. He's now en route to Dover himself. Out of the collision of these two erring old men who have been stripped naked and thrust over the borders of common experience into something rich, and strange, and terrible, Shakespeare will make one of the most powerful pieces of theater ever written. We shall look more closely at this encounter in my next lecture.

Timeline

Major Events in English Political History, the Theater, and Shakespeare's Life

1558 ....Elizabeth I comes to the throne.

1561–1562 ....*Gorboduc* (Thomas Sackville and Thomas Norton): first English play in blank verse.

1564 ....Birth of William Shakespeare.
Birth of Christopher Marlowe.

1569 ....Elizabeth quashes a major rebellion in the north of England led by supporters of her Catholic rival (and a claimant to the English throne), Mary Queen of Scots.

1576 ....James Burbage builds the first permanent playhouse (called The Theatre) on the south bank of the Thames. Eventually, seven playhouses are erected, but usually only two or three are in operation at any given time. Companies made up of young boys play at two indoor theaters.

1577 ....Francis Drake circumnavigates the globe.

1581 ....The Master of the Queen's Revels is empowered to approve (and censor) all plays intended for public performance.

1582 ....Shakespeare marries Ann Hathaway.

1583 ....Birth of Shakespeare's daughter Susanna.

1584–1585 ....Sir Walter Raleigh annexes Virginia for the English crown; failure of the Roanoke colony.

1585. ....Birth of Shakespeare's twin children, Hamnet and Judith.

1587 ....*Tamburlaine* (Christopher Marlowe).
The Spanish Tragedy (Thomas Kyd).

Execution of Mary Queen of Scots, mother of James VI of Scotland (who will later become James I of England).

1588 ....Defeat of the Spanish Armada (a large invasion fleet sent against England).

Late 1580s....................Shakespeare is now in London working as both an actor and a playwright.

1589–1593 ....Shakespeare's earliest plays, including *Henry VI*, parts 1, 2, and 3; *Richard III*; *Comedy of Errors*; *Love's Labor's Lost*; *Titus Andronicus*.

1592 ....*Doctor Faustus* (Christopher Marlowe).
First mention of Shakespeare by another author (insulting reference to him as an "upstart crow" in a pamphlet by Robert Greene).

1593 ....Marlowe killed in a tavern brawl.

1593–1594 ....Playhouses closed for many months because of a plague epidemic.
Shakespeare writes *Venus and Adonis* and *The Rape of Lucrece*.

1594–1600 ....Shakespeare writes some of his best known comedies and histories, including *A Midsummer Night's Dream*; *Merchant of Venice*; *As You Like It*; *Much Ado About Nothing*; *Richard II*; *Henry IV*, parts 1 and 2; and *Henry V*.

1594 ....Shakespeare listed as a joint stockholder of the acting company called the Lord Chamberlain's Men; he will remain with this company for the rest of his career.

1596 ....Death of Hamnet Shakespeare.
Romeo and Juliet.
Shakespeare successfully applies to the College of Heralds for a coat of arms for his family.

1597	Shakespeare buys New Place, the second largest property in Stratford (over the next decade, he purchases a significant amount of additional land in Stratford).
1598	Shakespeare listed as one of the "principal comedians" in Ben Jonson's *Every Man in His Humour*. Complimentary mention and listing of many of Shakespeare's plays in Francis Meres's *Palladis Tamia*.
1598–1599	The Globe Theatre is built for the Lord Chamberlain's Men. Used by the company until the closing of the theaters in 1642.
1599	*Julius Caesar*.
1600–1608	The Children of Saint Paul's (one of the "boys' companies") active on the indoor stage of Blackfriars Theatre.
1600–1601	*Hamlet*.
1601	Failed rebellion of the Earl of Essex, previously a favorite courtier of Elizabeth I.
1603	Death of Elizabeth I; James I succeeds to the throne. The Lord Chamberlain's Men become the King's Men.
1603–1604	Lengthy closure of the theaters because of plague epidemic.
1604	*Othello*.
1605	*King Lear*.
1605	Discovery of the Gunpowder Plot, a Catholic conspiracy to blow up the Houses of Parliament while King James was presiding.
1606	*Macbeth*.

Parliament passes an act to regulate and censor the language of stage plays.

1606–1607 .... *Antony and Cleopatra.*

1607 .... Captain John Smith settles Jamestown.

1607–1608 .... *Pericles.*

1608 .... *Coriolanus.*
Shakespeare listed as one of the joint owners of Blackfriars Theatre (where his company will now play during the winter months).

1609 .... Publication of Shakespeare's *Sonnets.*

1609–1610 .... *The Winter's Tale* and *Cymbeline.*

1610–1611 .... Shakespeare retires to Stratford.

1611 .... *The Tempest.*
Publication of the King James Version of the Bible.

1612–1613 .... *The Two Noble Kinsmen* (with John Fletcher).

1613 .... Destruction of the Globe by fire.

1614 .... Building of the second Globe.
Shakespeare involved in land disputes in Stratford.

1616 .... Death of Shakespeare.

1623 .... Publication of the First Folio of Shakespeare's plays (edited by his actor colleagues John Heminges and Henry Condell and entitled *Mr. William Shakespeare's Comedies, Histories and Tragedies*). It contains 36 plays, of which 18 had not been previously published.

1625 .... Death of James I; accession of his son Charles I.

1642 .... During the English Civil War, Parliament closes the theaters and bans public playacting. There is no public theater in England until the restoration of Charles II in 1660. None of the old playhouses survives the period of the Interregnum.

Glossary

agency: Most simply, the power to act freely and, by extension, to take responsibility for one's actions. In the imaginative universe of tragedy, characters often struggle to assert their agency in the face of forces (social, political, or metaphysical) that might inhibit their desires; alternatively, they may speak in ways that mystify or deny their agency, their responsibility for their deeds.

amphitheaters or public theaters (such as the Globe Theatre used by Shakespeare's company): Large buildings erected outside the city limits of London from the 1570s on for the performance of plays. They were polygonal in shape and had a stage that thrust out into an area where the "groundling" spectators might stand; one could pay a higher price to sit in galleries surrounding the yard. The original Globe had room for about 3,000 people. By contrast, *hall theaters* or *private theaters* (such as Blackfriars) were smaller, enclosed playing spaces in which performances did not take place only in natural light and where none of the audience stood. Seats were considerably more expensive in these theaters, and the companies who played in them originally consisted entirely of boy actors.

anagnorisis: Aristotle's term for a moment of charged recognition in a tragic plot.

aside: A remark made by a character speaking to himself or herself while in the company of others and, by convention, not heard by anybody else on stage.

blank verse: The verse form in which many Elizabethan and Jacobean dramatists composed much of their plays. It consists of unrhymed lines and is usually structured as iambic pentameter: that is, its rhythmical base consists of five groups of two syllables, in each of which an unstressed syllable is followed by a stressed syllable (dee-DUM). A skilled poet will, however, offer many variations on this basic pattern.

body politic: The state imagined as an organic system comparable to the human body—the image is common in the political philosophy of Shakespeare's day.

catharsis: Aristotle's term for a tragedy's emotional effect on its audience—in particular, its power to purge the strong emotions (especially pity and fear) that it has created in the spectator.

chorus: In classical Greek drama, the chorus was a group of actors not directly involved in the action who, at intervals, offered a commentary on what was unfolding on the stage. In Shakespeare's day, the "chorus" is a single actor who sometimes speaks the prologue of a play.

conceit: In early modern usage, a concept or idea or thought or image.

courtesan: A high-priced and rather high-class prostitute (Venice was famous for its courtesans).

dramatic irony: The term *irony* refers to words (or perhaps a situation) in which two levels of meaning are held in tension; when dramatic irony is at work, the audience, because its members have knowledge of a situation or of a character's actions or intentions that goes beyond that of other characters on the stage, perceives a special resonance in what is done or said that is unavailable to the characters over whom they hold the discrepancy of awareness.

Elizabethan: Pertaining to the period when Elizabeth I was ruler of England (1558–1603).

enjambement (sometimes spelled *enjambment*): We see enjambement in a poetic text when a line of verse does not stop syntactically at its typographical end but continues over the line break to complete itself in the next lines; a very common phenomenon in blank verse.

equivocation: To equivocate is to speak in a manner that is deceptive or ambiguous or involves the conscious deployment of double meanings (cf. the witches in *Macbeth*).

foil: A character positioned to provide contrast with another character. For example, Laertes-as-revenger is a foil to Hamlet-as-revenger.

folio: A large and expensive book format in which the sheets of printing paper that make up the work are folded just once. The first collected edition of Shakespeare's plays (published in 1623) used this format and is usually referred to as the First Folio.

Fortune: The personification of the principle of chance as it affects human events. "Lady Fortune" was often depicted as turning a wheel on which characters might rise (in prosperity, fame, or happiness) but would necessarily fall again.

gender: A term that points to identities that are socially constructed as "masculine" or "feminine" (as opposed to a merely biological definition of one's sex). Lady Macbeth, for example, "genders" compassion and pity as (problematically) feminine characteristics when asking the spirits of darkness to rid her of these emotions.

genre: Literary genres are different kinds or categories of literary works (for example, comedy, tragedy, epic); fairly specific artistic conventions (or audience expectations) are associated with given genres.

hamartia: Aristotle's term for the "error in action" that dooms a tragic protagonist; "tragic flaw" is an inadequate translation of this term.

honor: This word has a particular inflection in Shakespearean English when it is attached to a woman. It refers to her virginity (if she is unmarried) or her absolute sexual fidelity (if she is married).

interiority: The inner psychological state of a character—in Shakespearean drama, it is most obviously disclosed by way of the soliloquy (or, more briefly, by way of an aside).

Jacobean: Pertaining to the reign of James I of England (who was also James VI of Scotland); James ruled from 1603–1625.

Moor: Term used in the late 16th and early 17th centuries to describe any North African, whether Arab or sub-Saharan.

providential design: *Providence* is a term associated with Christian theology; it encompasses the notion of divine guidance or care. If one believes in a providential design, one believes that people act within a universe in which life is patterned and shaped in a meaningful way by a loving deity and in which their choices and actions have their own significance in the "big picture."

purgatory: In Roman Catholic doctrine, a place for the punishment and purification of the souls of those who had died in a state of grace: an intermediary stage before admission to heaven.

Puritans: Radical members of the Protestant faith. English Puritans wanted to reform the Anglican faith (the official and moderate version of Protestantism upheld by the monarchy after 1558) and move it even further away from the doctrine and ritual practices of Catholicism.

quarto: An inexpensive book format used to publish single plays; the name refers to the fact that a quarto was sewn together from multiple large sheets of printing paper folded twice to produce "gatherings" of four double-sided pages. Quite a few of Shakespeare's plays exist in individual quarto editions.

revenge tragedy: A type of tragedy first made popular by Elizabethan dramatists, in which the protagonist takes it upon himself to enact revenge for crimes his own society is unwilling to recognize or unable to punish. Such plays tend to involve the corruption of the revenger by his murderous pursuits and the bloody deaths of many characters.

Senecan tragedy: Tragedies written during the Elizabethan period in imitation of plays written by the Roman poet Seneca. Seneca's plays were written in five acts, were characterized by both emotional and physical violence (although the latter took place offstage in his works), and were prone to rhetorical extravagance. There is a significant overlap between Senecan tragedy and revenge tragedy.

soliloquy: A speech delivered by a character while alone on stage; characters often examine their feelings or reflect upon or interrogate their actions in soliloquy.

theater of the absurd: Drama that depicts the absurdity of the human condition; it usually questions conventional theological or philosophical ways of explaining or ordering the universe. In absurdist drama, isolated and usually powerless characters struggle to make sense of a bewildering cosmos. Samuel Beckett's *Waiting for Godot* (1954, English version) is a famous example of this kind of drama.

tragedy of fate: A tragedy in which the actions of the protagonists are represented as being predetermined to a considerable degree by larger metaphysical forces.

tragedy of state: A tragedy with a good deal of overt political content, in which the actions of the characters will determine the fate of a state or realm. The proper uses (and the abuses) of power are often debated in the action.

tragic knowledge: The special insight or vision sometimes granted to the tragic protagonist: perception clawed from supreme suffering. It is possible, to be sure, that the "knowledge" achieved by this character might be interrogated by audience members who hold a larger awareness of the complete action of a play.

tragic protagonist: The central character in a tragedy. Not necessarily the "tragic hero" (protagonists aren't necessarily male, and tragic protagonists may, in fact, be officially villains—e.g., Macbeth).

transgression: In tragedy, this might be equated with Aristotle's "error in action," but the term has the specific sense of an action that separates one from ordinary experience and puts one "beyond the pale." The definition of "transgressive" behavior is not necessarily an absolute one: it is often socially determined, for example, when Brabantio deplores Desdemona's "unnatural" act of marrying Othello.

virtus: Latin word that is roughly equivalent to "virtue" but also has gendered connotations of specifically "manly" behavior: courage, the faithful performance of public responsibilities to the state, and so on (cf. Cominius's public commendation of Coriolanus).

Shakespeare: A Biographical Note

William Shakespeare was born in the provincial town of Stratford-upon-Avon in 1564, the eldest son of John Shakespeare and Mary Arden. John Shakespeare's father had been a small farmer, a tenant of Mary's prosperous landowning family; he himself was, for many years, a thriving glove-maker and tanner who held several important official positions in local administration, including that of alderman. When William was about 12, his father's business went into decline and John Shakespeare was no longer active in civic affairs: he accrued heavy debts and defaulted on a mortgage he had taken out on a tract of land that was part of his wife's inheritance. He appears, however, to have recovered his respectability in later years, perhaps aided by his financially successful son. In 1596, an application made by William for the Shakespeares to be granted their own coat of arms was approved by the College of Heralds; this would have officially marked the family as "gentry."

William Shakespeare did not attend university, but as the son of a respectable tradesman, he would have been educated for up to 10 years at the quite prestigious local grammar school. *Grammar* here means Latin grammar: William would have read the works of Cicero, Seneca, Virgil, and Ovid and would have had some training in rhetoric and oratory. He might also have had his first exposure to theater during these years: records show that traveling companies of players quite regularly performed in Stratford.

It is not clear what trade or profession Shakespeare followed between leaving school and moving to London. We do know that in November 1582, at the age of 18, he married Anne Hathaway, who was 8 years his senior. Anne was already pregnant; Shakespeare's daughter Susanna was born 6 months after the marriage. In 1585, Anne gave birth to the twins Judith and Hamnet (Hamnet would die young in 1596). No records have been found of Shakespeare's doings from this point until his arrival in London, although it has been suggested that he found employment as a country schoolmaster. In his *Groats-Worth of Wit* (1592), Robert Greene, surveying the literary scene in London, mocks "an upstart Crow" who, with "his Tygers hart wrapt in a Players hyde, supposes he is as well able to bombast out a blanke verse" and "is in his owne conceit the onely Shake-scene in a countrey." Greene here parodies a line taken from

Shakespeare's very early play *Henry VI*, part 3; it is clear from his remarks that Master "Shake-scene" was already quite well known, both as an actor and as a dramatist.

Our most detailed knowledge of Shakespeare's London career comes after 1594, when he became a "sharer," or joint stockholder, in the company of players called the Lord Chamberlain's Men (all acting companies had to have the patronage of a person of rank or risk being prosecuted as "rogues and vagabonds"). We do know that his long narrative poems *Venus and Adonis* and *The Rape of Lucrece* were written just prior to this, when the London theaters were closed for more than a year because of a plague epidemic. After 1594, Shakespeare wrote exclusively for the Lord Chamberlain's Men until his retirement, usually finishing two plays per year. He continued to act from time to time, and we know he participated in performances of works by his learned contemporary Ben Jonson.

Until the turn of the century, Shakespeare mainly (although not exclusively) wrote history plays and romantic comedies; his works at this time include *A Midsummer Night's Dream*; *Romeo and Juliet*; *Much Ado About Nothing*; *The Merchant of Venice*; *As You Like It*; *Richard II*; *Henry IV*, parts 1 and 2; and *Henry V*. In *Palladis Tamia: Wit's Treasury* (1598), a contemporary commentator, Francis Meres, praises Shakespeare's dramatic art and approvingly lists 12 of his plays. The playwright seems to have remained in London for much of this time, although he presumably visited Stratford during the winter when the public theaters were closed. He invested much of his earnings in Stratford properties, beginning in 1597 with his purchase of New Place, considered the second most impressive house in his hometown. In 1607, when Susanna Shakespeare married a local physician, her father was able to give her a considerable marriage settlement that included more than 100 acres of land.

In 1599, the Lord Chamberlain's Men moved to the newly built Globe Theatre, the company's main home for the remainder of Shakespeare's career. All the major tragedies discussed in this course were first performed in the Globe, although in 1608, Shakespeare's company also acquired shares in the private hall theater of Blackfriars. After James I came to the English throne in 1603, the Lord Chamberlain's Men were given royal patronage and renamed the King's Men; from then on, the company quite often performed at court, as well as at the Globe or Blackfriars.

In the final stage of his career, Shakespeare produced complex hybrids of comedy and tragedy—plays whose striking use of spectacle may have exploited the superior technical facilities of the Blackfriars Theatre. In these later years, Shakespeare renewed his Stratford ties and, around 1610–1611, seems to have moved back there on a more permanent basis. (In 1614, he was embroiled in a legal case, involving the enclosure of land formerly held in common, that created significant local unrest.) Early in 1616, he drafted and then redrafted his will, showing particular care to protect the financial interests of his daughter Judith, who had recently married a man of dubious character. He made special bequests to just three of his colleagues in the King's Men and notoriously mentioned his wife only once, leaving her "my second best bed." (Anne may well have automatically received one-third of his estate as the "widow's portion," but the lack of even the most conventional terms of endearment in her husband's single reference to her is striking.) Shakespeare died on April 23, 1616, and was buried in Stratford's Holy Trinity Church: a verse on his tomb roundly curses anyone who disturbs his bones. Seven years after his death, John Heminges and Henry Condell, two of the three fellow players mentioned in his will, published the first (more or less) complete edition of his plays.

Bibliography

Primary Texts:

You should read Shakespeare in a good modern edition with notes and annotations. There are many complete editions of the plays, and the following are recommended.

The Norton Shakespeare: Based on the Oxford Edition, edited by Stephen Greenblatt, Walter Cohen, Jean Howard, and Katharine E. Maus. New York: W.W. Norton & Co., 1997. (This edition is used by the lecturer and includes a very good general introduction.)

The Complete Works of Shakespeare, edited by David Bevington, 4th ed. New York: Longman, 1997.

The Riverside Shakespeare, edited by G. Blakemore Evans, et al., 2nd ed. Boston: Houghton Mifflin, 1997.

There are many good scholarly editions of individual plays. Three particular series of such editions are well thought of by many experts in the field: the *Arden Shakespeare: Third Series* (published by Thomas Nelson), the *Oxford Shakespeare*, and *The New Cambridge Shakespeare*. All volumes in these series offer full introductions and exhaustive notes. The single volumes are published in both hardback and paperback. Especially recommended are the following single editions from these series (listed with the names of their editors):

Hamlet. Edwards, Philip (Cambridge, 2003). Hibbard, G. R. (Oxford, 1987).

Othello. Neill, Michael (Oxford, 2006). Sanders, Norman (Cambridge, 2003).

King Lear. Foakes, R. A. (Arden, 1997). Halio, Jay L. (Cambridge 1992, or updated edition of 2005).

Macbeth, Braunmuller, A. R. (Cambridge, 1997). Brooke, Nicholas (Oxford, 1990).

Antony and Cleopatra, Neill, Michael (Oxford, 1994).

Coriolanus, Bliss, Leo (Cambridge, 2000). Parker, R. B. (Oxford, 1994).

Note on variations among texts of Shakespeare's plays:

Some of Shakespeare's plays were not printed until his colleagues, Condell and Heminges, collected his works after his death in the

©2007 The Teaching Company.

volume we call the First Folio and which they entitled *Mr. William Shakespeare's Comedies, Histories and Tragedies* (1623). Others were printed in one or more individual editions (the *quartos*) before the First Folio appeared. We have no surviving manuscripts of any Shakespeare play and no information as to whether (in an era before copyright) Shakespeare himself was ever involved in the publication of any one of these earlier editions. There are some striking variations among the different texts. Hamlet, for example, wishes that his "too too solid flesh would melt" in the First Folio of his tragedy but wishes that his "too too sallied flesh would melt" in the first and second quarto editions of the play. A modern editor must often choose between different readings of the same line or even offer an interpretive correction when the printed text seems odd (so that some editors emend "sallied" to "sullied" and substitute this reading for the Folio's "solid"). *There is no single absolutely stable and "authorized version" of a Shakespeare play.* Indeed, one or two early editions, most notably the first quarto of *Hamlet*, are so wildly different from others that it has been suggested they were pirated versions based on the "memorial reconstruction" of an actor who performed in the work. If you find that a line or passage in your own text differs from that quoted by the lecturer, you may want to consult the textual notes of your edition to find out what is going on, in terms of editorial practice, at this point!

Other Primary Texts:

Christopher Marlowe's *Tamburlaine* and *Doctor Faustus*, along with Thomas Kyd's *Spanish Tragedy*, mentioned in Lecture Two, may be found in: *English Renaissance Drama*, edited by David Bevington, et al. New York: Norton, 2002.

Supplementary Reading:

Adelman, Janet. *Suffocating Mothers: Fantasies of Maternal Origin in Shakespeare's Plays*. New York: Routledge, 1992. Feminist psychoanalytic readings of mothers (absent and present) in Shakespeare's plays, with particular emphasis on the tragedies.

Bate, Jonathan. *The Genius of Shakespeare*. New York: Oxford University Press, 1998. A fine and capacious exploration of Shakespeare's life and writings—and of the qualities that have sustained his fame.

Bradley, A. C. *Shakespearean Tragedy: Lectures on Hamlet, Othello, King Lear, Macbeth.* 3rd ed. New York: St. Martin's, 1992. Originally published in 1904. A very influential work on Shakespearean tragedy: somewhat "Victorian" in nature but still interesting.

Briggs, Julia. *This Stage-Play World: Texts and Contexts, 1580–1625.* 2nd ed. New York: Oxford University Press, 1997. A lively and useful discussion of historical, social, and cultural contexts for reading Renaissance English literature.

Bullough, Geoffrey, ed. *Narrative and Dramatic Sources of Shakespeare.* 8v. London: Routledge & Kegan Paul, and New York: Columbia University Press, 1957–1975. Reproduces the sources of Shakespeare's plays and discusses the ways in which Shakespeare reshaped them. A good place to find the Thomas North translations of Plutarch that Shakespeare used in writing *Antony and Cleopatra* and *Coriolanus.*

Cantor, Paul. *Shakespeare's Rome: Republic and Empire.* Ithaca and London: Cornell University Press, 1976. A useful study of Shakespeare's remaking of Roman political history.

Cavell, Stanley. *Disowning Knowledge in Seven Plays of Shakespeare.* Cambridge: Cambridge University Press, 1987. A distinguished contemporary philosopher addresses Shakespeare. Includes fine essays on *Lear* and *Coriolanus.*

Danson, Lawrence. *Shakespeare's Dramatic Genres.* Oxford: Oxford University Press, 2000. A concise discussion of the main features of Shakespearean comedy, history, and tragedy.

Deats, Sara Munson, ed. *Antony and Cleopatra: New Critical Essays.* New York: Routledge, 2005. A collection of recent essays on the play.

De Grazia, Margaret, and Stanley Wells, eds. *The Cambridge Companion to Shakespeare.* Cambridge: Cambridge University Press, 2000. A reference anthology that has some particularly interesting chapters on contemporary and global responses to Shakespeare's work.

Dollimore, Jonathan. *Radical Tragedy.* Chicago: University of Chicago Press, 1984. This provocative "new historicist" reexamination of Renaissance tragedy, which includes an excellent chapter on *King Lear*, pays particular attention to the political resonances of early-modern theater.

Drakakis, John, ed. *Shakespearean Tragedy*. New York, Longman, 1992. An anthology of essays on the plays (with an emphasis on recent theoretical approaches) that also includes a preliminary chapter offering an overview of major discussions of tragedy across the last 200 years.

Greenblatt, Stephen. *Hamlet in Purgatory*. Princeton: Princeton University Press, 2002. A rich and suggestive discussion of the treatment of death, mourning, and the role of the Ghost in *Hamlet* within the context of the religious debates of the English Reformation.

Gurr, Andrew. *The Shakespearean Stage, 1574–1642*. 3rd ed. Cambridge: Cambridge University Press, 1992. Solid resource for information about the playhouses and players in Shakespeare's era.

Kahn, Coppelia. *Roman Shakespeare: Warriors, Wounds and Women*. New York: Routledge, 1997. Feminist/historicist study of Shakespeare's Roman plays.

Kerrigan, John. *Revenge Tragedy: Aeschylus to Armageddon*. Oxford: Clarendon Press, 1996. A wide-ranging, recent study of this subgenre in all its manifestations.

Kirsch, Arthur. *The Passions of Shakespeare's Tragic Heroes*. Charlottesville: University Press of Virginia, 1990. A sensitive humanist reading of the plays.

Kott, Jan. *Shakespeare Our Contemporary*. New York: Norton, 1974. An iconoclastic account of Shakespeare originally dating from the 1960s and still provocative; some fine essays on the tragedies.

Lockyer, Roger. *James VI and I*. London and New York: Longman, 1998. A concise history of the reign of Elizabeth I's successor.

Mangan, Michael. *A Preface to Shakespeare's Tragedies*. London and New York: Longman, 1991. Helpful introductory chapters on Shakespeare's theater and on literary trends in the early 17th century; later chapters offer intelligent overviews of the plays.

McDonald, Russ. *The Bedford Companion to Shakespeare: An Introduction with Documents*. 2nd ed. Boston and New York: Bedford, 2001. A helpful reference book with excellent chapters on a variety of historical, social, theatrical, and literary contexts for reading the plays. Includes some trenchant pages on the authorship question.

————, ed. *Shakespeare: An Anthology of Criticism and Theory, 1945–2000*. Oxford: Blackwell, 2004. A wide-ranging anthology of well-chosen examples of various schools of Shakespeare criticism.

Neely, Carol Thomas. *Broken Nuptials in Shakespeare's Plays*. Urbana and Chicago: University of Illinois Press, 1993. Contains her groundbreaking essay "Women and Men in *Othello*."

Neill, Michael. *Issues of Death: Mortality and Identity in English Renaissance Tragedy*. Oxford: Clarendon Press, 1997. Substantial and learned discussions of the tragedies.

Poole, Adrian. *Tragedy: A Very Short Introduction*. New York: Oxford University Press, 2005. Concise, accessible, and historically wide-ranging survey of tragedy as a literary genre.

Schoenbaum, Samuel. *William Shakespeare: A Compact Documentary Life*. Rev. ed. New York: Oxford University Press, 1987. Perhaps the single best resource for biographical information about Shakespeare.

Sinfield, Alan, ed. *Macbeth*. New York: St. Martin's, 1992. Collection of recent critical essays on *Macbeth*, with a particular emphasis on new historicist interpretations.

Snyder, Susan. *The Comic Matrix of Shakespeare's Tragedies*. Princeton: Princeton University Press, 1979. Examines the ways in which plot structures and conventions from Shakespeare's comedies are reshaped in the tragedies; suggestive discussion of *Othello*.

Young, David, ed. *Shakespeare's Middle Tragedies: A Collection of Critical Essays*. Englewood Cliffs, NJ: Prentice Hall, 1993. A short anthology of some of the most influential recent articles on *Hamlet*, *Othello*, and *Lear*. Highly recommended.

Internet Resources:

Internet Shakespeare Editions, http://ise.uvic.ca/Foyer/index.html. Superb (and visually beautiful) reference site. Many links to well-presented material about Shakespearean contexts; excellent online reference for the plays themselves (elegantly scanned in multiple editions). You can search the texts or browse scene by scene. Includes an excellent Shakespeare-in-Performance database and many links to further reading.

Shakespeare Resource Center, http://www.bardweb.net. Extremely accessible and easy-to-navigate site that offers links to essays and illustrations on a good range of topics (for example, "The Globe Theatre" or "Elizabethan England"), followed by an annotated set of links to aid further research.

Films and Videos:

Following is a selected list of TV films and movies, available on video or DVD, that the lecturer has found of interest.

Hamlet

- 1948 film version directed by and starring Laurence Olivier. Black and white. Hamlet as a supremely introspective and wounded Renaissance man. Very marked cuts (Rosencrantz and Guildenstern, for example, disappear completely).

- 1980 made-for-TV film, part of the BBC/Time-Life series of all the Shakespeare plays. Directed by Rodney Bennett. Mainly remarkable for a superb performance by Derek Jacobi as the prince.

- 1990 film version directed by Franco Zeffirelli; Mel Gibson as Hamlet. Glenn Close is first-rate as Gertrude, and the closet scene is very sexually charged.

- 1996 version directed by and starring Kenneth Branagh. The whole text is filmed (or at least *a* whole text is filmed!). Updated to what looks like 19th-century Germany. Derek Jacobi is a fine Claudius, and Branagh, an interestingly aggressive prince.

- 2000 version directed by Malcolm Almereyda and starring Ethan Hawke. Contemporary setting; Hamlet is an independent filmmaker.

Othello

- 1952 version directed by Orson Welles (who plays the lead). The film was made in bits and pieces and varies wildly in quality, but some parts of it are visually astonishing.

- 1995 version directed by Oliver Parker with Laurence Fishburne as Othello and Kenneth Branagh as a nastily cheerful Iago. Some interesting moments, but the play is too drastically cut.

King Lear

- 1971 film directed by Peter Brook based on his celebrated stage production of some years before. Famously idiosyncratic—and a particularly brutal version of the play. Paul Scofield is a very fine Lear.

- 1983 or 1984 made-for-TV version of the play directed by Michael Elliot and starring an old and frail (although still, at times, astonishing) Laurence Olivier, whose own physical fragility gives the play extra poignancy. A superb cast; a gentler version of the play than the Brook film.

- 1998 film directed by the acclaimed Richard Eyre with Ian Holm as a tough, difficult Lear: recommended.

Macbeth

- 1948 film by Orson Welles shot quickly and on the cheap. Extremely horrible costumes. Welles is occasionally powerful as Macbeth.

- 1971 film version by Roman Polanski, made (in)famous by Lady Macbeth sleepwalking naked. Some visually astonishing moments (the opening sequence in which a battle is evoked on the misty margins of the sea is splendid), but the acting tends to be bland.

- 1978 filmed-for-TV version of a studio theater production by the Royal Shakespeare Company, directed by Philip Casson, based on original direction by Trevor Nunn. Possibly the best film of any Shakespearean tragedy; Ian McKellen and Judi Dench are superb as Macbeth and his lady, and the claustrophobic filming style is beautifully fitted to the play.

Antony and Cleopatra

- Film directed by Jon Scofield, based on a famous 1974 Royal Shakespeare Company production. Richard Johnson and Janet Suzman offer fine performances as Antony and Cleopatra; a young Patrick Stewart is an interesting Enobarbus.

Notes

Notes